The

Mammals
of Southern Africa

Burger Cillié

Dedication

To my father (Vadie)

Burger Cillié

SUNBIRD PUBLISHERS

This edition first published in 2003
Third edition 2004
Reprinted in 2005, 2006
Fourth edition 2007
Reprinted in 2008, 2009
Fifth edition 2010
Reprinted in 2011, 2012, 2013

Sunbird Publishers (Pty) Ltd
P O Box 6836, Roggebaai, 8012 Cape Town, South Africa

www.sunbirdpublishers.co.za

Registration number 1984/003543/07
Copyright © published edition 2003 Sunbird Publishers
Copyright © text 2010 Burger Cillié

Copyright © photography 2010 Burger Cillié,
Unless credited otherwise on page 144
Cover photograph Lizeth Cillié
Title page photograph Niel Cillié

(First published as *Pocket-guide to Southern African Mammals*
by J.L. Van Schaik Publishers, 1992)

Publisher Ceri Prenter
Designer Guineafolio
Project manager Cherie Wright
Copy editor Sean Fraser
Illustrator Annelise Burger

Reproduction by Resolution, Cape Town, South Africa
Printed and bound by Craft Print International Ltd, Singapore

ISBN: 978-1-920289-23-2

Contents

Introduction

The format of this book has been chosen so that it can fit into your pocket, and has been compiled to serve as a manual for quick identification of not only the animals, but also of their spoor. Reliable sketches of the spoor and photographs of dung facilitate identification. Where the sexes of individual animals differ visually, both are illustrated by means of photographs.

All the species featured in this guide are found in the geographical area south of the Kunene and Zambezi rivers, while a key to the habitat in which they are found provides easy cross referencing to where they may be discussed in this guide. Maps also show the distribution of the mammals and their subspecies.

For the trophy hunter, minimum requirements as well as the latest records according to the Rowland Ward (R.W.) and Safari Club International (S.C.I.) systems are provided.

This pocket-sized guide will be ideal for the hunter, hiker and nature lover.

Vegetation:
Simplified map of southern Africa

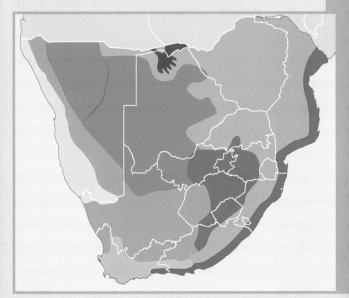

Habitat keys

Only six of the most important vegetation regions in southern Africa are discussed. These are the bushveld (savannah), the Kalahari, the highveld grasslands, the Karoo, fynbos, and the Damaraland bushveld of Namibia. The river/marshes and surrounding floodplains of the Okavango and Caprivi have also been included because of the unique occurrence of certain antelope.

Each region has been divided into a number of typical habitat types. The species that occur in these regions are listed in columns beneath the habitat types on the following pages. These keys should be used as an aid towards fast and accurate identification of animals and as an indication of the habitat where certain species may occur.

■ Coastal forest
■ Highveld grassland
■ Kalahari
■ Karoo
■ Fynbos

■ Damaraland bushveld
■ Bushveld
  Desert
■ Okavango/Caprivi

Bushveld (savannah)

Antelope

Thicket	Plain	Marsh	River	Koppie
Greater kudu	Blue wildebeest	Buffalo	Buffalo	Greater kudu
Nyala	Tsessebe	Lichtenstein's hartebeest	Nyala	Eland
Red duiker	Roan antelope	Waterbuck	Waterbuck	Common duiker
Blue duiker	Sable antelope	Reedbuck	Red duiker	Klipspringer
Duiker	Buffalo	Oribi	Blue duiker	Mountain reedbuck
Suni	Kudu	Steenbok	Impala	Bushbuck
Lichtenstein's hartebeest	Eland	Impala	Duiker	Sharpe's grysbok

Bushveld (savannah)

Larger predators

Thicket	Plain	Marsh	River	Koppie
Side-striped jackal	African wild dog	African civet	Side-striped jackal	Black-backed jackal
African civet	Side-striped jackal	Aardwolf	African civet	Brown hyaena
Spotted hyaena	Black-backed jackal		Spotted hyaena	Leopard
Leopard	Aardwolf		Leopard	Lion
Cheetah	Brown hyaena		Lion	
Lion	Spotted hyaena			

Bushveld (savannah)

Smaller predators

Thicket	Plain	Marsh	River	Koppie
Large-spotted genet	Small-spotted genet	Caracal	Large-spotted genet	Caracal
Serval	Caracal	Yellow mongoose	African wild cat	Striped polecat
African wild cat	African wild cat	Dwarf mongoose		Slender mongoose
Striped polecat	Striped polecat	**Marsh and river**		Honey badger
Banded mongoose	Yellow mongoose	Small-spotted genet	Serval	
Honey badger	Slender mongoose	Spotted-necked otter	African clawless otter	
	Dwarf mongoose	Honey badger	White-tailed mongoose	
		Marsh mongoose	Banded mongoose	

Bushveld (savannah)

Other larger mammals

Thicket	Plain	Marsh	River	Koppie
Baboon	Baboon	Elephant	Baboon	Baboon
Black rhinoceros	Elephant	White rhinoceros	Elephant	Giraffe
Bushpig	Plains zebra	Black rhinoceros	Black rhinoceros	Porcupine
Giraffe	White rhinoceros	Antbear	Antbear	Porcupine
Ground pangolin	Antbear	Warthog	Bushpig	Hippopotamus
Porcupine	Common warthog	Bushpig	Giraffe	
	Giraffe	Hippopotamus	Ground pangolin	

Bushveld (savannah)

Other smaller mammals

Thicket	Plain	Marsh	River	Koppie
South African hedgehog	South African hedgehog	Springhare	South African hedgehog	Vervet monkey
Greater galago	South African galago	Greater cane rat	Greater galago	Rock hyrax
South African galago	Cape hare		South African galago	Tree squirrel
Vervet monkey	Tree squirrel		Vervet monkey	Scrub hare
Syke's monkey	Springhare		Syke's monkey	Tree squirrel
Scrub hare	Tree squirrel		Scrub hare	Greater cane rat

Okavango and Caprivi

Swamp/river and floodplains

Antelope

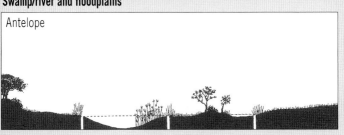

River bank	River	Flooded area	Dry floodplain
Bushbuck	Sitatunga	Waterbuck	Oribi
Reedbuck	Steenbok	Red lechwe	Impala
Waterbuck	Duiker	Steenbok	Reedbuck
Impala		Tsessebe	Waterbuck
Greater kudu			Puku

Highveld grassland

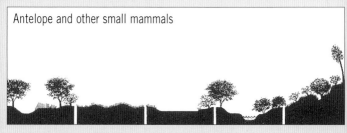

Antelope and other small mammals

Stream	Grassplains	Pan	River	Koppies and mountains
Blesbok	Black wildebeest	Springhare	Duiker	Duiker
Duiker	Blesbok		South African hedgehog	Klipspringer
Steenbok	Oribi		Scrub hare	Oribi
South African hedgehog	Steenbok	South African hedgehog	Springhare	Grey rhebok
Ground squirrel	Scrub hare	Cape hare	Vervet monkey	Mountain reedbuck
	Vervet monkey			Rock hyrax

Highveld grassland

Predators and other large mammals

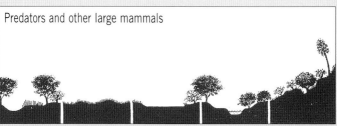

Stream	Grassplains	Pan	River	Koppies and mountains
African wild cat	Aardwolf	Aardwolf	African wild cat	Slender mongoose
Striped polecat	Caracal	Caracal	White-tailed mongoose	Brown hyaena
Small-spotted genet	Small spotted cat	Suricate (meerkat)	Marsh mongoose	Baboon
Slender mongoose	Striped polecat	Yellow mongoose	Baboon	Rock hyrax
White-tailed mongoose	Yellow mongoose	Marsh mongoose	Small-spotted genet	Striped polecat
Marsh mongoose	Suricate (meerkat)	Black-backed jackal	Cape fox	White rhinoceros
White rhinoceros	Cape fox	White rhinoceros	Black-backed jackal	Antbear

Kalahari

Antelope

Dry river	Dune land	Plain	Pan
Blue wildebeest	Red hartebeest	Blue wildebeest	Springbok
Duiker	Springbok	Red hartebeest	Duiker
Springbok	Steenbok	Springbok	Steenbok
Steenbok	Duiker	Steenbok	Gemsbok
Gemsbok	Gemsbok	Duiker	
Greater kudu	Greater kudu	Gemsbok	
Eland	Eland		

Kalahari

Other mammals

Dry river	Dune land	Plain	Pan
Antbear	Antbear	Antbear	Springhare
Common warthog	Ground pangolin	Common warthog	
Ground pangolin	Scrub hare	Ground pangolin	
Cape hare	Porcupine	Cape hare	
Scrub hare	Springhare	Ground squirrel	
Ground squirrel	Porcupine	Springhare	Porcupine

Kalahari

Predators

Dry river	Dune land	Plain	Pan
Bat-eared fox	Honey badger	Bat-eared fox	Cape fox
African wild dog	Bat-eared fox	Black-backed jackal	Aardwolf
Black-backed jackal	African wild dog	Aardwolf	Suricate (meerkat)
Small-spotted genet	Cape fox	Spotted hyaena	Yellow mongoose
Aardwolf	Black-backed jackal	Cheetah	Caracal
Brown hyaena	Small-spotted genet	Yellow mongoose	Small-spotted genet

Kalahari

Predators (continued)

Dry river	Dune land	Plain	Pan
Spotted hyaena	Brown hyaena	Suricate (meerkat)	Yellow mongoose
Cheetah	Spotted hyaena	Lion	African wild cat
Leopard	Cheetah	Caracal	Striped polecat
Lion	Leopard	Small spotted cat	Slender mongoose
Caracal	Striped polecat	Yellow mongoose	Yellow mongoose
African wild cat	Suricate (meerkat)	Slender mongoose	

Damaraland bushveld

Antelope

Pan and floodplains	Woodland	Thicket	Stream/river	Koppie
Blue wildebeest	Blue wildebeest	Duiker	Duiker	Duiker
Red hartebeest	Red hartebeest	Damara dik-dik	Black-faced impala	Klipspringer
Springbok	Springbok	Black-faced impala	Greater kudu	Damara dik-dik
Steenbok	Steenbok	Greater kudu	Eland	Greater kudu
Gemsbok	Black-faced impala	Gemsbok		Eland
	Gemsbok	Greater kudu		

Damaraland bushveld

Other mammals

Pan and floodplains	Woodland	Thicket	Stream/river	Koppie
Plains zebra	Elephant	Baboon	Elephant	Baboon
Antbear	Plains zebra	Elephant	White rhinoceros	Mountain zebra
Common warthog	White rhinoceros	Black rhinoceros	Black rhinoceros	Porcupine
Ground pangolin	Antbear	Giraffe	Antbear	Scrub hare
Ground squirrel	Common warthog	SA hedgehog	Common warthog	Vervet monkey
Spring hare	Giraffe	Vervet monkey	Scrub hare	Scrub hare
Porcupine	Ground pangolin	Spring hare		

Damaraland bushveld

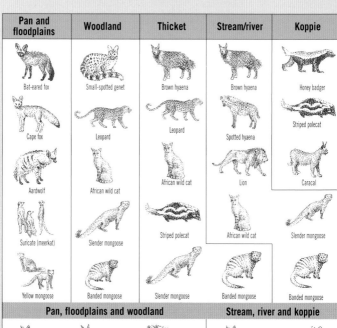

Pan and floodplains	Woodland	Thicket	Stream/river	Koppie
Bat-eared fox	Small-spotted genet	Brown hyaena	Brown hyaena	Honey badger
Cape fox	Leopard	Leopard	Spotted hyaena	Striped polecat
Aardwolf	African wild cat	African wild cat	Lion	Caracal
Suricate (meerkat)	Slender mongoose	Striped polecat	African wild cat	Slender mongoose
Yellow mongoose	Banded mongoose	Slender mongoose	Banded mongoose	Banded mongoose

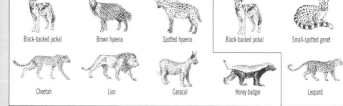

Pan, floodplains and woodland			Stream, river and koppie	
Black-backed jackal	Brown hyaena	Spotted hyaena	Black-backed jackal	Small-spotted genet
Cheetah	Lion	Caracal	Honey badger	Leopard

Fynbos

Predators

Coastal plain	River	Plateau	Mountain slope
Bat-eared fox	Black-backed jackal	Bat-eared fox	Large-spotted genet
Cape fox	Large-spotted genet	Cape fox	Leopard
Black-backed jackal	Leopard	Black-backed jackal	African wild cat
Small-spotted genet	Small-spotted genet	Small-spotted genet	Striped polecat
Aardwolf	African wild cat	Aardwolf	Honey badger
Caracal	Striped polecat	African clawless otter	Caracal	Striped polecat
Honey badger	Yellow mongoose	Honey badger	Marsh mongoose	Yellow mongoose

Fynbos

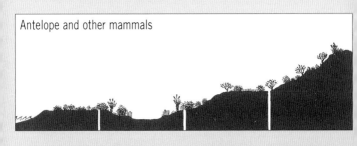

Antelope and other mammals

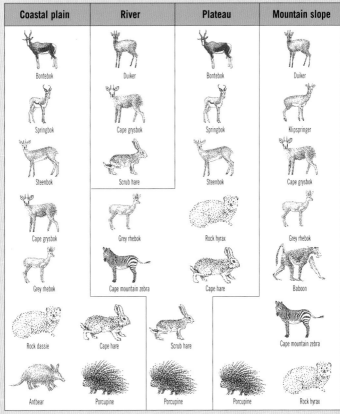

Coastal plain	River	Plateau	Mountain slope
Bontebok	Duiker	Bontebok	Duiker
Springbok	Cape grysbok	Springbok	Klipspringer
Steenbok	Scrub hare	Steenbok	Cape grysbok
Cape grysbok	Grey rhebok	Rock hyrax	Grey rhebok
Grey rhebok	Cape mountain zebra	Cape hare	Baboon
Rock dassie	Cape hare	Scrub hare	Cape mountain zebra
Antbear	Porcupine	Porcupine	Porcupine	Rock hyrax

Karoo

Antelope and other mammals

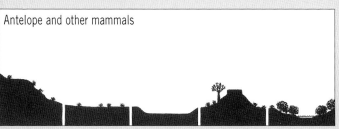

Mountain slope	Plain	Pan	Koppie	Stream/river
Duiker	Springbok	Springbok	Klipspringer	Duiker
Klipspringer	Steenbok	Gemsbok	Greater kudu	Steenbok
Grey rhebok	Gemsbok	Cape hare	Mountain reedbuck	Greater kudu
Greater kudu	Ground squirrel	Antbear	Cape mountain zebra	Baboon
Mountain reedbuck	Cape hare	Scrub hare	Rock hyrax	Vervet monkey
Baboon	Rock hyrax	Porcupine	Antbear	Black rhinoceros
Cape mountain zebra	Cape hare	Porcupine	Scrub hare	Ground squirrel

23

Karoo

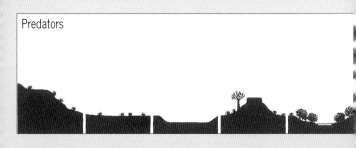

Predators

Mountain slope	Plain	Pan	Koppie	Stream/river
Black-backed jackal	Bat-eared fox	Bat-eared fox	Black-backed jackal	African clawless otter
Striped polecat	Cape fox	Cape fox	Honey badger	Honey badger
Caracal	Black-backed jackal	Aardwolf	Striped polecat	Marsh mongoose
White-tailed mongoose	Aardwolf	Suricate (meerkat)	African wild cat	African wild cat
Caracal	Honey badger	Caracal		
Small spotted cat	Striped polecat	Small spotted cat		
	Suricate (meerkat)			

South African hedgehog

Atelerix frontalis
(Suid-Afrikaanse krimpvarkie)

Subspecies

▪ *A.f. frontalis*
▪ *A.f. angolae*

Identification The upper parts of the body are covered with black and white or dull yellow ringed spines. The white-framed face ends in a pointed snout.

Difference between ♂ and ♀ None.

Habitat Dry shelter for nests, and enough insects and other food are essential. Occurs in a variety of habitats in bush savannah and grassland. Avoids moist soil. Independent of water.

Habits Mainly nocturnal, but also appears during the day, especially after rain, to feed on earthworms (which move to the surface) and insects. Becomes torpid during winter. Rests during the day in piles of debris or in holes, changing resting places daily. The only semipermanent nests are those used by females to nurse a litter, and during winter when hibernating. Poor eyesight, but keen sense of smell to locate food just below the surface.

Food Mainly millipedes, centipedes, beetles, termites, moths, locusts and earthworms. Sometimes also chicks of small ground-living birds, small mice, lizards, birds' eggs, snails, frogs and fungi. Drinks water when available.

Breeding 1–9 young are born October–April after a gestation period of ±5 weeks. ♀ has 2 pairs pectoral and 1 pair abdominal mammae.

Mass
236–480 g

Length
±20 cm

Age
±3 years

Vocalisation
High-pitched alarm; snorts, sniffs and growls when they meet.

25

Greater galago

Otelemur crassicaudatus
(Bosnagaap)

Mass
♂ ±1.22 kg, ♀ ±1.13 kg

Length
♂ ±74 cm, ♀ ±73 cm

Age
Unknown

Vocalisation
Repeated ominous hoarse wailing, which may be heard over a considerable distance, slightly resembling a child crying. Alarm call: a shrill scream.

Subspecies

▬ *O.c. crassicaudatus* (slightly reddish brown on back)

■ *O.c. monteiri* (upper parts yellowish, under parts ash grey)

Identification The largest of the two bushbabies. Huge eyes and broad, rounded mobile ears. The fur is long and soft, especially at the tail.

Differs from other species South African galago: smaller, fur less fluffy and tail not as thick. Utilises different habitat types.

Difference between ♂ and ♀ The male is slightly larger than the female.

Habitat Mountain forest, forest and dense woodland in areas with a high rainfall. Found even in riverine forest surrounded by arid country, such as Gauteng and the surrounding areas.

Habits Nocturnal: appears after sunset and is periodically active at night. First grooms itself after appearing. Gregarious – usually found in family groups that rest high up in thick foliage during the day. Forages alone, urinates on its feet and hands and also rubs chest glands against branches and other bushbabies as a means of scent-marking its home range.

Food Fruit such as wild figs, mobola plums and kudu-berries. Also gum, insects and, occasionally, birds and reptiles.

Breeding Usually 2 young are born August–September (November in northern regions) after a gestation period of ±4 months. ♀ has 1 pair pectoral and 1 pair groin mammae.

26

South African galago

Subspecies

G.m. moholi (greyish brown, with ash-grey underparts)

G.m. bradfieldi (brownish, with more yellowish underparts)

Identification Huge eyes; the large ears are membranaceous and very mobile. The tail is long and the fur fluffy.

Differs from other species Greater galago: larger, with longer, softer fur, especially on tail. Different habitat. Similar to the yellowish Grant's galago *Galagoides grantii*, previously part of *G.m. bradfieldi*, which occur in parts of Zimbabwe and Mozambique.

Difference between ♂ and ♀ The male is slightly larger.

Habitat A savannah species: prefers mopane and especially acacia savannah along rivers and tributaries. Thorn trees shelter numerous insects and supply gum, both of which are essential for its diet. Old thorn and mopane tree trunks have hollows that serve as shelter for bushbabies. Independent of water.

Habits Mainly nocturnal: active during the first and last part of the night. Small groups rest during the day in nests or holes in trees; at night individuals forage on their own. Dominant animals in particular urinate on their hands and feet and also rub their chest glands against other bushbabies. They can take huge leaps while moving from tree to tree.

Food Gum is essential, as are insects such as locusts, moths, beetles and spiders. Does not take in water – gets enough liquid in diet.

Breeding 1–2 (sometimes 3) young are born October–November and/or January–February after a gestation period of just over 4 months.

Mass
♂ ±155 g, ♀ ±150 g

Length
♂ ±37 cm, ♀ ±36 cm

Age
±10 years

Vocalisation
Growl, low-pitched alarm call, and birdlike *cheek-cheek* noises.

Chacma baboon

Papio hamadryas ursinus
(Kaapse bobbejaan)

♂

♀

Mass
♂ 27–44 kg, ♀ 14–17 kg

Shoulder height
♂ ±71 cm, ♀ ±61 cm

Age
±18 years

Vocalisation
Males have a bisyllabic bark; the others chatter and shriek.

Subspecies The Chacma baboon is now a subspecies of the Hamadryas baboon.

Identification Long legs and an elongated face, with eyes close together. Has pink callosities and a sickle tail.

Difference between ♂ and ♀ The male is larger and more aggressive than the female.

Habitat Prefers cliffs or tall trees for shelter, and also sufficient water for drinking. Consequently, prefers mountains, hills, riverine forests and various types of savannah with enough food.

Habits Troops vary from about 20 animals with one dominant male to 100 with 12 dominant males. These adult males are prominent in most of the activities: troop movement, chasing and fighting, mating, grooming, guarding and maintaining a strict hierarchy. They forage during the day, leaving their sleeping sites just after sunrise and returning in the late afternoon.

Food Grass, leaves, bulbs, roots, gum, wild fruit, mushrooms, berries, scorpions, snails, insects and meat. Drinks water regularly.

Breeding 1 (seldom 2) young are born throughout the year after a gestation period of ±6 months. ♀ has 1 pair of pectoral mammae.

16 cm

Vervet monkey

Cercopithecus aethiops
(Blouaap)

C.a. pygerythrus

C.a. cloetei

Subspecies

- *C.a. pygerythrus* (greyish, olive sheen)
- *C.a. helvecens* (yellow on back, pale legs)
- *C.a. marjoriae* (pale, light ash grey)
- *C.a. ngamiensis* (pale feet, yellowish back)
- *C.a. ruforviridis* (dull, reddish-brown back)
- *C.a. cloetei* (darker greyish-brown speckles, dark feet)

Identification Small, black face, a conspicuous long tail ending in a dark-brown tip; male's scrotum is blue.

Differs from other species Syke's monkey: larger and browner, with black legs and shoulders.

Difference between ♂ and ♀ The male is larger than the female.

Habitat Savannah species: prefers fairly dense savannah – the ecotone between savannah and forest and riverine forest, even if surrounded by unfavourable terrain. Water, sufficient fruit-bearing trees and trees for shelter are requirements.

Habits Troops consist of up to 20 animals with an apparent hierarchy. The higher in social ranking, the more readily they are recognised. They have a strong sense of coherence, which is reinforced by mutual grooming. They sleep in tall trees and forage early in the morning and again later in the afternoons, returning to their sleeping sites well before sunset.

Food Wild fruit: jackalberry, wild figs, marula and sourplum. Pods of camel-thorn and mopane, as well as gum, birds' eggs and insects.

Breeding 1 (rarely 2) young are born throughout the year after a gestation period of ±7 months. ♀ has 1 pair of pectoral mammae.

Mass
♂ 3.8–8.0 kg, ♀ 3.4–5.2 kg

Shoulder height
♂ ±31 cm, ♀ ±26 cm

Age
±12 years

Vocalisation
Chatters or stutters as an alarm call. Young also squeal.

Syke's monkey

Cercopithecus mitis
(Samango-aap)

♂

♀

Mass
♂ 8.2–10 kg, ♀ 4.5–5.2 kg

Shoulder height
♂ ±39 cm, ♀ ±35 cm

Age
Unknown

Vocalisation
Boom and repeated *nyah* sounds are heard most often.

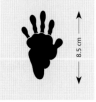
8.5 cm

Subspecies
■ *C.m. labiatus*
■ *C.m. erythrarchus*

Identification Legs, shoulders and end part of the tail are black. Hind legs are very long, and the body slants forward when all four feet are on the ground.

Differs from other species Vervet monkey: smaller, more greyish, with a black face. Male scrotum is blue.

Difference between ♂ and ♀ The male is larger than the female.

Habitat Prefers dense coastal forest, mountain forest and riverine forest (even dry forest) – leaves this habitat in search of food only, or when moving to another habitat. Dense forest with tall trees for shelter and trees that provide food are essential.

Habits Troops vary between 4 (with 1 adult male) and 34 (with 3 or more adult males). Sleeps in tall trees at night and forages intermittently during the day. Basks in the morning sun before going out to forage. Usually rests during the heat of the day. The males guard the troop when it moves out. Mutual aggression occurs.

Food Gum of thorn trees, leaves, berries, shoots, soft seed pods, wild fruit, caterpillars and other insects.

Breeding 1 young is born September–April after a gestation period of ±4 months. ♀ has 1 pair of pectoral mammae.

African wild dog

Lycaon pictus
(Wildehond)

Subspecies None.

Identification Dog-like animals with rounded ears. The coats have white, yellow, brown and black blotches. The latter half of the tail is white.

Differs from other species Spotted hyaena: larger, with black/brown spots and no white. Sloping back; tail is shorter and dark brown, and ears are smaller.

Difference between ♂ and ♀ None.

Habitat Prefers grass plains or open woodland, and avoids thickets and tall grass. Requires open areas, and availability of its principal food is essential. Relatively scarce in areas containing large numbers of lions and spotted hyaenas. Independent of water.

Habits Gregarious – hunts in packs, chases prey and tears it apart while still running. Also feeds the rest of the pack by regurgitating some of the meat when returning to the den. Lives in packs of 10–15; packs of up to 40 have been recorded. Diurnal: hunts in early morning or afternoon.

Food Anything from scrub hare and lambs to kudu and blue wildebeest, especially impala and springbok. Drinks water when available.

Breeding 7–10 (even 19) pups born March–July after a gestation period of ±2 months. ♀ has 6 or 7 pairs of mammae.

Mass
20–32 kg

Shoulder height
±68 cm

Age
±10 years

Vocalisation
Excited chattering and a well-known *who-who* sound.

8.5 cm

Mass
♂ ±2.8 kg, ♀ ±2.5 kg

Shoulder height
±33 cm

Age
Unknown.

Vocalisation
A bark and high-pitched crying sound.

Subspecies None.

Identification Small built, light brown to silverish grey; large ears and broad, bushy tail with a black tip.

Differs from other species Bat-eared fox: larger, darker in colour, with black limbs and large ears. Black-backed jackal: large, red-brown with dark 'saddle'.

Difference between ♂ and ♀ The male is slightly heavier than the female.

Habitat Open grassland with patches of shrubs and open, dry thornveld of Karoo shrubveld. Less frequent in open bushveld and Cape fynbos. Frequents grassland around dry pans in Botswana. Independent of water.

Habits Solitary, quite asocial and never groom one another. Mainly nocturnal: active periods are just before sunrise and just after sunset. Rests in holes or tall grass during daytime. Digs its own shelter or adapts an old springhare hole. As home areas overlap, it defends only a small territory around the hole in which young are raised.

Food Smaller mammals (especially mice). Also insects, spiders, reptiles and birds.

Breeding 1–5 young are born October–November after a gestation period of ±2 months. ♀ has 1 pair groin and 2 pairs of abdominal mammae.

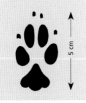

Bat-eared fox

Otocyon megalotis
(Bakoorvos)

Subspecies Only one subspecies occurs in this region:
▪ *O.m. megalotis*

Identification Very large rounded ears, bushy tail with black tip, fluffy coat; the lower parts of the legs are black.

Differs from other species Cape fox: lighter build, lighter in colour (light brown), especially the legs, and has a silvery sheen. The ears are smaller.

Difference between ♂ and ♀ The female is slightly heavier than the male.

Habitat Found in arid areas, open grass plains, open woodland with short grass and bare patches, as well as scattered shrubveld in the Karoo. The presence of harvester termites is essential. Independent of water.

Habits Occurs in pairs or small family groups of up to 6. Nocturnal and diurnal, usually resting during the heat of day in holes, patches of tall grass or beneath shrubs. Keen hearing: digs up underground larvae by listening to their movements. Owing to its skill in twisting and turning at high speed, it was given the Afrikaans name of 'draaijakkals' ('turning jackal').

Food Mainly insects such as harvester termites, locusts and larvae. Also scorpions, mice, reptiles, wild fruit, spiders and millipedes.

Breeding 2–6 young are born September–November after a gestation period of ±2 months. ♀ has 2 pairs of groin mammae.

Mass
♂ 3.4–4.9 kg, ♀ 3.2–5.3 kg

Shoulder height
±30 cm

Age
±12 years

Vocalisation
Who–who crying sound. A sharp knocking sound by young ones in distress.

4 cm

Side-striped jackal

Canis adustus
(Witkwasjakkals)

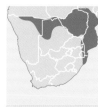

Mass
♂ 7.3–12 kg, ♀ 7.3–10 kg
Shoulder height
±39 cm

Age
±11 years

Vocalisation
A series of short *nyah-nyah* sounds, the first *nyah* not as drawn out as that of the black-backed jackal.

Subspecies Only one subspecies occurs in this region:

■ *C.a. adustus*

Identification A white stripe on the flanks (sometimes also a dark stripe below), which leads to its name 'side-striped'. The bushy tail ends in a white tip.

Differs from other species Black-backed jackal: reddish on the flanks and legs; has a dark 'saddle' on the back.

Difference between ♂ and ♀ The male is slightly heavier than the female.

Habitat Usually in well-watered areas. Generally prefers woodland, thickets, valleys and thickly wooded areas. Avoids open grass plains, forests and mountainous areas. Dependent on water.

Habits More nocturnal than black-backed jackal; active during greatest part of the night and sometimes seen just before sunset and after sunrise. Solitary, although pairs or mother with young are sometimes seen. Rests during the day under a cairn or in old antbear holes.

Food Carrion, wild fruit (such as wild figs), scrub hares, mice, moles, insects, birds and lizards.

Breeding 2–6 young are born August–January after a gestation period of 2–2½ months. ♀ has 2 pairs of groin mammae.

34

Black-backed jackal

Canis mesomelas
(Rooijakkals)

Subspecies Only one subspecies occurs in this region:

▇ *C.m. mesomelas*

Identification Light reddish brown (cf. Afrikaans name: 'Rooijakkals'). The 'saddle' on its back is black with white speckles.

Differs from other species Side-striped jackal: a white stripe (sometimes also a dark stripe below) on the flanks; the tail ends in a white tip.

Difference between ♂ and ♀ The male is slightly heavier.

Habitat Utilises a variety of habitat types that provide sufficient food. Prefers open arid areas such as woodland or grassland with enough shrubs. In Botswana, it avoids the well-watered areas in the north (Okavango). Independent of water.

Habits Diurnal and nocturnal; mainly seen at sunset and sunrise. Although they are usually solitary, they live in pairs and establish a territory. Both the male and female defend and mark this area. They are scavengers and gather around a carcass. Rests during the day in old antbear holes, between rocks or in cliffs. Shy and cunning with a keen sense of smell.

Food Carrion, lambs, mice, hares, springhare, locusts, crickets, beetles, termites and wild fruit. Can stay without water, but drinks when it is available.

Breeding 1–6 (rarely 9) young are born July–October after a gestation period of ±2 months. ♀ has 2 pairs of groin mammae.

Mass
♂ 6.8–11.4 kg, ♀ 5.5–10 kg

Shoulder height
±38 cm

Age
±13 years

Vocalisation
A drawn-out *nyah-nyah* sound, interspersed with short *nya-nya* sounds.

5.5 cm

35

African clawless otter

Aonyx capensis
(Groototter)

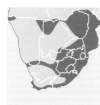

Mass
10–18 kg

Length
±130 cm

Age
±15 years

Vocalisation
A high-pitched scream,
aggressive hiss and growl and
a contented purring sound.

Subspecies Only one subspecies occurs in this region:
▇ *A.c. capensis*

Identification Aquatic. A long, broad tail and a large, broad head.
The throat and the sides of the face under the eyes and ears are white.

Differs from other species Spotted-necked otter: has claws on all
four feet; white spots on the throat and lacks the white on the throat
and sides of face.

Difference between ♂ and ♀ None.

Habitat Rivers, lakes, swamps, dams, streams and even the sea.
Aquatic areas with enough food and an environment offering
adequate shelter to rest in is essential. Wanders further from water
than the spotted-necked otter.

Habits Usually solitary – diurnal and nocturnal – especially at
twilight. Rests in dry shelter or among reeds when it is warm.
Spends a great part of its life in water. Usually swims on the surface,
but can also dive for long periods. After swimming, it will lie in
the sun to dry.

Food Mainly frogs and crabs, but also fish, octopuses, insects, birds
and reptiles. Fish are eaten head first, while the spotted-necked otter
starts at the tail.

Breeding 1 (sometimes 2) young is born throughout the year after a
gestation period of ±9 weeks. ♀ has 2 pairs of pectoral mammae.

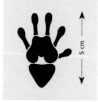

5 cm

Spotted-necked otter

Lutra macullicollis
(Kleinotter)

Subspecies

■ *L.m.macullicollis* (South east) (chestnut-brown)
■ *L.m.chobiensis* (seal-brown)

Identification The body is long and slim, and the long tail is flattened below. The toes are webbed with short claws on every toe. The fur is soft and there are white spots against the throat and upper chest.

Differs from other species African clawless otter: is larger and stockier in build. The throat and sides of the face are white.

Difference between ♂ and ♀ Males are bigger than females.

Habitat Restricted to larger lakes, dams, rivers and marshes with large stretches of open water and shelter like thickets and reeds close by. Avoids estuaries and seawater.

Habits Single or in small groups of up to 5 members. They are diurnal, with a peak in activity early in the morning and late in the afternoon. More confined to water than the African clawless otter; leaving the water only to rest or to excrete. Clumsy on land. They use latrines, usually on the grass, close to the water's edge. Swim gracefully even in rough water at rapids. They swallow fish tail first.

Food Fish, crabs and frogs; sometimes also insects and birds.

Breeding 1–2 (sometimes 3) young are born from November–December. ♀ has 2 pairs of abdominal mammae.

Mass
♂ ±4.5kg, ♀ ±3.5 kg

Length
±97 cm

Age
Unknown

Vocalisation
Unknown

Honey badger

Mellivora capensis
(Ratel)

Mass
7.9–14.5 kg

Shoulder height
±26.5 cm

Age
±24 years

Vocalisation
A high-pitched bark. Growls and grunts, and also makes a nasal *harr-harr* type of sound.

Subspecies Only one subspecies occurs in this region:

■ *M.c. capensis*

Identification Stocky build with short legs. Upper parts of the body are whitish-grey to light brown, and the rest of the body is black. Skin is loose, thick and very tough.

Difference between ♂ and ♀ None.

Habitat Occurs in a variety of habitat types, and even in very arid parts. Prefers open areas on rocky hills, in shrubby sandveld, grassland, open woodland, scattered riverine forests and floodplains, such as around the Okavango swamps. Avoids mountain forests and deserts. Independent of water.

Habits Mainly nocturnal, but often seen during the day. Generally solitary, but also seen in pairs. Very brave and will even attack animals larger than itself. Rests during the day and hunts at night. Moves with a rolling gait, with its snout held close to the ground. The small honeyguide sometimes leads it to a bees' nest.

Food Very fond of honey and bee larvae, but also eats meat, scorpions, fruit, birds, insects, reptiles, mice and even spiders.

Breeding Usually 2 young are born October–January after a gestation period of ±6 months. ♀ has 2 pairs of groin mammae.

8.5 cm

Striped polecat

Ictonyx striatus
(Stinkmuishond)

Subspecies None.

Identification Parallel black and white bands along its back. The body and tail have long hair. White patches below the ears.

Differs from other species Striped weasel: smaller, with shorter hair and sinuous body; lacks the white patches below the ears.

Difference between ♂ and ♀ The male is larger.

Habitat Adaptable; utilises many habitat types, but never abundantly. Found along dry streams running through deserts, in shrubveld to open grassland, open woodland, thorn thickets, on rocky hills, in forests. Independent of water.

Habits Usually solitary, seldom in pairs. Nocturnal: appears only well into the night. Moves sinuously. Digs its own shelter in soft soil, but usually takes shelter in old springhare holes, rock piles or fallen tree logs. When disturbed, stands on its hind legs to observe the area. Uses well-known, unpleasant and nauseating exudation as its last resort in defence.

Food Mainly mice and insects. Also birds, frogs, reptiles, scorpions, spiders and millipedes.

Breeding 1–3 young are born October–March after a gestation period of 5–6 weeks. ♀ has 1 pair of abdominal and 1 pair of groin mammae.

Mass
♂ 681–1460 g, ♀ 593–880 g

Shoulder height
±10 cm

Age
±8 years

Vocalisation
Growls and barks.

2.5 cm

Small-spotted genet

Genetta genetta
(Kleinkolmuskejaatkat)

Mass
±19 kg

Shoulder height
±15 cm

Age
±12 years

Vocalisation
Growls and spits.

2.5–3 cm

Subspecies

▤ *G.g. felina* (black spots)

▨ *G.g. pulchra* (reddish-brown spots)

Identification Very small and cat-like, with a long body and short legs. The long tail has black rings ending in a white tip.

Differs from other species Large-spotted genet: larger spots on the body, white chin and tail ends in a black tip.

Difference between ♂ and ♀ None.

Habitat Occurs in open arid areas, where large-spotted genet are absent. Prefers woodlands with open grasslands or dry marshes, riverine forests and dry shrubby woodland. Needs enough shelter, such as shrubs, undergrowth and holes in the ground or in trees for resting. Independent of water.

Habits Exclusively nocturnal. Mainly solitary, but also seen in pairs. It is terrestrial but also is a keen tree climber when hunting or seeking shelter. Rests in holes in the ground during the day (where there are no trees). Runs fast, with its head down and tail held horizontally.

Food Insects such as beetles and locusts, mice and rats, spiders, snakes and birds.

Breeding 2–4 young are born August–April after a gestation period of 10–11 weeks. ♀ has 2 pairs of abdominal mammae.

Large-spotted genet and common large-spotted genet

Genetta tigrina/G. maculata
(Grootkolmuskejaatkat/
Rooikolmuskejaatkat)

Common large-spotted genet

Species This species is now divided into two species (as named above). *Genetta maculata* replaces *G.t. rubiginosa*, a former subspecies.

■ *G. tigrina* (large black spots, hind feet black) Large-spotted genet
■ *G. maculata* (spots and stripes more rusty brown)

Identification Very small and cat-like, with a long body, short legs and a long black banded tail ending in a black tip.

Differs from other species Small-spotted genet: long dark crest on the back, dark chin, and the tail ends in a white tip.

Difference between ♂ and ♀ None.

Habitat Prefers riverine forests and woodlands and, in contrast to the small-spotted genet, usually avoids open plains or dry marshes. Occurs more generally in well-watered areas with a high rainfall (450+ mm/annum). Dependent on water.

Habits Exclusively nocturnal and appears only long after sunset. Rests during the day in holes in trees, tree trunks or in old antbear or springhare holes. Mainly solitary, and usually walks slowly and stealthily. When disturbed or hunting, it takes to the trees and leaps for distances of up to 4 metres from tree to tree. It sometimes stands on its hind legs to observe the surroundings.

Food Mice, locusts, beetles, crickets, spiders, scorpions, frogs, centipedes and wild fruit.

Breeding 2–5 young are born August–March after a gestation period of ±2 months. ♀ has 2 pairs of abdominal mammae.

Mass
1.4–3.2 kg

Shoulder height
±15 cm

Age
±13 years

Vocalisation
Growls and spits.

2.5–3 cm

African civet

Civettictis civetta
(Afrikaanse siwet)

Mass
♂ 9.5–13.2 kg, ♀ 9.7–15 kg

Shoulder height
±40 cm

Age
±12 years

Vocalisation
Usually silent. A loud cough-like bark, a low threatening growl, a scream when fighting and a low *woof* sound.

5.5 cm

Subspecies
▤ *C.c. australis*
▦ *C.c. volkmanni*

Identification Cat-like, with whitish-grey body and black spots merging to stripes on the hindquarters. Black around the eyes, with white spots on either side of the nose.

Difference between ♂ and ♀ The female is slightly heavier than the male.

Habitat Prefers areas with sufficient undergrowth, trees and shrubs bearing fruit that lure insects. Requires enough shelter, such as tall grass, wooded areas, thickets (especially with palms) and reeds. Found more frequently where there is permanent water.

Habits Exclusively nocturnal and very shy; active for a period after sunset and also at sunrise. Not a very keen tree climber – depends on fruit falling down naturally or as a result of the actions of other animals or birds. Mainly solitary; uses footpaths that are also used by other civets and deposits its excreta in latrines next to the paths. Stands quite still or lies down flat when disturbed. Acute senses of smell and hearing.

Food Insects, wild fruit, reptiles, birds and frogs.

Breeding 1–4 young are born August–December after a gestation period of ±2 months. ♀ has 2 pairs of abdominal mammae.

Suricate (Meerkat)

Suricata suricatta
(Stokstertmeerkat)

Subspecies

▤ *S.s. suricatta* (darker, dark brown around the eyes)

▤ *S.s. marjoriae* (paler, stripes on back, lighter around the eyes)

Identification Round head with a short, pointed nose and distinctive slender, tapering dark-tipped tail. Dark rings around the eyes and dull dark bands on the lower back.

Differs from other species Ground squirrel: a distinctive white stripe on the flanks and the bushy tail has long hair.

Difference between ♂ and ♀ None.

Habitat Open arid areas. Prefers hard or calcareous soil in which to dig its burrows. In the Northern Cape, it frequents the banks of dry pans. Avoids mountainous areas. Independent of water.

Habits Diurnal: only appearing from its hole once the sun has reached it, after which it will sunbathe for a while. Playful and lives in colonies of up to 20 animals, usually occupying a burrow dug by ground squirrels, or sometimes sharing it with ground squirrels or yellow mongooses.

Food Worms, insect larvae, small snakes, snake eggs, lizards, spiders, scorpions, centipedes and millipedes.

Breeding 2–5 young are born October–March after a gestation period of 10–11 weeks. ♀ has 3 pairs of abdominal mammae.

Mass
620–960 g

Length
±50 cm

Age
±12 years

Vocalisation
Loud bark as alarm call, constant grunting while foraging.

Yellow mongoose

Cynictus penicillata
(Witkwasmuishond)

Mass
440–900 g

Length
±55 cm

Age
±12 years

Vocalisation
Unknown

Subspecies
A gradient complex – a gradual physical change occurs within the species, with the following as the two extremes:
■ *C.p. cinderella* (smaller, grey, short tail without white tip)
■ *C.p. penicillata* (larger, yellow, long white tip to the tail)
Identification Colour varies from yellow- or reddish-brown with a white-tipped tail or greyish without the white tail tip.
Differs from other species Selous mongoose: smaller, nocturnal and the last three-quarters of the tail is white. Slender mongoose: tail is less bushy and ends in a black tip.
Difference between ♂ and ♀ None.
Habitat Open plains in the Karoo, grass plains of the Free State, semidesert shrubby veld in Botswana and grass plains in Namibia. In woodland, it prefers open grass patches such as those around water holes. Independent of water.
Habits Mainly diurnal and forms colonies of 20 or more animals. Often shares burrows with ground squirrels and/or suricates, but can dig its own burrow. Forages further away from its burrow than the other two species and makes use of temporary shelter in case of emergency.
Food Beetles, beetle larvae, termites, mice, insects, crickets, caterpillars, ants, locusts, birds, reptiles and ground-living birds.
Breeding 2–5 young are born October–March after a gestation period of ±8 weeks. ♀ has 3 pairs of abdominal mammae.

2.75 cm

Slender mongoose

Galerella sanguinea
(Swartkwasmuishond)

G.s. sanguinea

G.s. ratlamuchi

A new species, Kaokoland slender mongoose *Galerella flavescens* (completely black), replaces the former subspecies *G.s. nigrata* from Namibia.

Subspecies

▮ *G.s. sanguinea* (greyish brown to yellowish grey)

▮ *G.s. ratlamuchi* (orange-red; long hair; dark tail tip)

Identification Solitary. Colour varies from reddish-brown to dark brown and grey. The tail is very long and thin, and has a black tip turning upwards.

Differs from other species Yellow mongoose: gregarious; its tail is bushier and usually ends in a white tip. Meller's mongoose: tail is much shorter and the hair is much longer. Sometimes has a black tail.

Difference between ♂ and ♀ The male is larger than the female.

Habitat Not choosy in its habitat requirements. Usually found in open areas to woodlands and even up to the edge of forests. Prefers areas with sufficient shelter, such as anthills, rocks or holes in hollow tree trunks.

Habits Mainly solitary and diurnal, becoming active when it is warmer. Although terrestrial, it can climb trees when hunting or frightened. Usually moves quickly, using footpaths. Freezes or stands up on its hind legs when disturbed in order to investigate.

Food Locusts, termites, beetles, ants, lizards, mice and wild fruit.

Breeding 1–2 young are born October–March. ♀ has 1–3 pairs of abdominal mammae.

Mass
♂ ±640 g, ♀ ±460 g

Length
±60 cm

Age
±8 years

Vocalisation
Silent. Young make a *hee-nwhe* sound.

2.5 cm

45

Cape grey mongoose

Galerella pulverulenta
(Kleingrysmuishond)

G.p. ruddi

Mass
±500–1000 g

Length
±55–69 cm

Age
Unknown

Vocalisation
Unknown

Subspecies
- *G.p. pulverulenta* (pale grey)
- *G.p. basutica* (darker grey)
- *G.p. ruddi* (more brownish)

Identification Similar to the slender mongoose – which replaces this species to the north – but is more grey (black with white speckles).

Differs from other species Slender mongoose: more brown to reddish brown, with a thinner, black-tipped tail.

Difference between ♂ and ♀ The male is slightly larger than the female.

Habitat Found in various habitats, from forests and fynbos regions to arid areas with sparse vegetation and even in mountainous habitats.

Habits Solitary (sometimes in pairs) and diurnal, but less active during the warmer parts of the day. Mainly terrestrial, but sometimes hunts in trees. Uses holes in termite heaps or stacks of rocks for shelter if suitable vegetation is not available. Not afraid of humans.

Food Insects, birds, reptiles, mice and carrion.

Breeding 1–3 young are born August–December in a breeding burrow. ♀ has 3 pairs of abdominal mammae.

5.5 cm

White-tailed mongoose

Ichneumia albicauda
(Witstertmuishond)

Subspecies Only one species occurs in this region:

▉ *I.a. grandis*

Identification A very large mongoose. Black legs, long tail with long white hair for the last four-fifths of length.

Differs from other species Selous mongoose: smaller, and a smaller part of the tail is white. Meller's mongoose: sometimes has a white tail, but a brown body.

Difference between ♂ and ♀ The male is slightly heavier than the female.

Habitat Occurs generally in well-watered woodland up to the edge of mountain forests; also found in more arid areas, and along rivers and swamps such as the Okavango delta. Prefers more humid types of woodland. Dependent on water.

Habits Nocturnal: active well after sunset but only until midnight. Rests during the day in old antbear or springhare holes. Terrestrial: seldom climbs trees; rather makes use of thickets or holes for shelter when chased. Usually solitary, although pairs and family groups are also seen.

Food Termites, beetles, locusts, crickets, frogs, mice, lizards, snakes, wild fruit and earthworms.

Breeding 1–3 young are born September–December. ♀ has 3 pairs of abdominal mammae.

Mass
♂ ±4.5 kg, ♀ ±4.1 kg

Length
±1.1 m

Age
Unknown

Vocalisation
Unknown

4 cm

Marsh mongoose

Atilax paludinosus
(Watermuishond)

Mass
2.4–4.1 kg

Shoulder height
±15 cm

Age
±11 years

Vocalisation
Growls and makes a
high explosive bark.

Subspecies Only one subspecies occurs in this region:

▪ *A.p. paludinosus*

Identification A large mongoose. It is dark brown and has white cheeks and a large, broad head. Long hair (especially on the tail).

Differs from other species White-tailed mongoose: lighter in colour with black legs and distinctive white tail.

Difference between ♂ and ♀ None.

Habitat Generally found in well-watered areas – especially near rivers, dams, streams, swamps, marshes and estuaries; prefers a dense shelter in reed patches or reeds on higher ground out of reach of floodwaters. Found in dry areas along waterways such as the Okavango and Gariep. Dependent on water.

Habits Mainly solitary. Active for about 2 hours before dark and 3 hours after first light, but for longer periods on overcast days. Uses paths on the muddy sides of water in search of food. Keen swimmer, and takes to the water when in danger.

Food Frogs (such as clawed frogs), crabs, marsh rats, mice, insects, insect larvae, mussels and prawns.

Breeding 1–3 young are born August–December. ♀ has 3 pairs of abdominal mammae.

Banded mongoose

Mungos mungo
(Gebande muishond)

♂ *M.m. taenianotus*   ♀ *M.m. grisonax*

Subspecies

M.m. grisonax (light grey with reddish sheen, and brown bands on the back)

M.m. taenianotus (darker reddish brown, with black bands on the back)

Identification Characteristic feature is the dark, transverse bands from mid-back to the base of the tail.

Difference between ♂ and ♀ None.

Habitat Prefers areas along rivers and marshes, as well as dry thornveld and other thickets with sufficient trees, undergrowth, fallen logs and anthills. Fond of riverine forests along the Zambezi, Limpopo and other large rivers. Independent of water.

Habits Forms colonies varying from a few animals up to 30 or more. Move far apart when foraging, but maintain contact by continuous twittering. All freeze and some stand on their hind legs when an alarm call is given. Although terrestrial, they sometimes take shelter in trees. Diurnal and sleep in old antbear holes or holes in anthills.

Food Insects, larvae, millipedes, snails, lizards, frogs, snakes, scorpions, spiders, locusts, birds' eggs, chickens, beetles, crickets, ants and wild fruit. Drinks water when available.

Breeding 2–8 young are born October–February after a gestation period of ±8 weeks. ♀ has 3 pairs of abdominal mammae.

Mass
1.0–1.6 kg

Shoulder height
±12.5 cm

Age
±8 years

Vocalisation
Twittering and a loud crack sound as an alarm call.

3 cm

Dwarf mongoose

Helogale parvula
(Dwergmuishond)

Mass
210–340 g

Shoulder height
±7.5 cm

Age
±6 years

Vocalisation
Perrip and *chuck* sounds
to keep contact. Alarm call is
a *shu-shwee* sound.

Subspecies
■ *H.p. parvula* (dark brown)
☰ *H.p. nero* (black)
■ *H.p. mimetra* (lighter, rusty brown)

Identification A very small mongoose. At a distance, the colour seems dark brown or black, but from nearby one can see its white speckles.

Difference between ♂ and ♀ None.

Habitat A savannah species. Prefers dry open woodland or grassveld in which there are areas of hard or stony soil containing fallen trees, anthills and other plant material. Anthills are essential for shelter. Independent of water.

Habits Diurnal: becomes active long after sunrise and returns to its sleeping site long before sunset. Lives in groups of 8–10, but groups of up to 30 have been spotted. An anthill is usually the permanent shelter of such a group. They sometimes dig their own hole, placing the entrance beneath a fallen log. Keep contact with one another while foraging by constantly making *chuck* sounds.

Food Insects, insect larvae, termites, snails, locusts, crickets, scorpions, centipedes, caterpillars, earthworms, lizards, snakes, mice and moth larvae.

Breeding 2–4 young are born October–March after a gestation period of ±8 weeks. ♀ has 3 pairs of abdominal mammae.

Aardwolf

Proteles cristatus
(Aardwolf)

Subspecies Only one subspecies occurs in this region:

■ *P.c. cristatus*

Identification Sloping back, 4–5 transverse black stripes on the flanks and a few stripes on the legs. Has a mane of long hair.

Differs from other species Brown hyaena: larger, darker in colour and lacks the stripes on the flanks. Spotted hyaena: larger, has spots and no stripes.

Difference between ♂ and ♀ None.

Habitat Utilises a large variety of plant habitats; generally found in dry areas (100–600 mm/annum). Prefers open areas such as dry marshes, grass plains and open patches around pans. Found only where there are sufficient termites.

Habits Nocturnal: rests during the day in old antbear or other holes, which it adapts for itself. Solitary. Does not take carrion, and feeds mainly on termites. Roars and growls loudly and mane bristles when confronted. Dangerous canine teeth are seldom used. Uses glands above anus to mark its presence.

Food Termites and other insects, with harvester termites being the most important. Sometimes feeds on spiders, moths, centipedes and ants, but not on meat.

Breeding 2–4 young are born September–April after a gestation period of ±2 months.

Mass
7.7–13.5 kg

Shoulder height
±50 cm

Age
±13 years

Vocalisation
Growl ending in a sudden bark. Loud roar when under stress.

5.5 cm

Brown hyaena

Parahyaena brunnea
(Bruinhiëna)

Mass
♂ 35–57 kg, ♀ 28–48 kg

Shoulder height
♂ ±79 cm, ♀ ±76 cm

Age
±24 years

Vocalisation
Growls, snorts and yelps. Whines and squeals as a sign of submissiveness.

Subspecies None.

Identification Sloping back, a light-brown neck, with a light-brown mantle on the shoulders. The legs have lighter rings.

Differs from other species Spotted hyaena: ears are rounded, hair is much shorter, colour is yellowish with dark spots. Aardwolf: much smaller and of lighter colour, with transverse stripes.

Difference between ♂ and ♀ The male is larger than the female.

Habitat Generally found in arid areas. In Gauteng and surrounds, it prefers mountainous areas or dry mopane veld, and scavenges on the beach at night in Namibia. Uses shelters such as holes, branches of trees near the ground, thick shrubs or patches of grass.

Habits Mainly nocturnal: solitary, but is attached to a group with a fixed territory. Rests during the day beneath shrubs or in holes. The group scent-marks its area and makes use of communal dung heaps near the boundaries of its territory.

Food Mainly carrion. Seldom hunts, but will feed on small animals such as springhares, mongooses, reptiles and ground-living birds.

Breeding 1–5 young born August–November after a gestation period of 3 months. ♀ has 1 pair of abdominal mammae.

9–10 cm

Spotted hyaena (Laughing hyaena)

Crocuta crocuta
(Gevlekte hiëna)

Subspecies None.

Identification Sloping back, with very strong neck and forequarters. Dark spots on the body become duller with age.

Differs from other species Brown hyaena: darker in colour, with longer hair and more pointed ears. Aardwolf: smaller, with transverse stripes and no spots.

Difference between ♂ and ♀ The female is slightly larger than the male.

Habitat Savannah species: dependent on the presence of antelope. Found in riverine-type savannah, but prefers open plains and woodland. Dependent on water.

Habits Usually single or 2–3 together belonging to a group of up to 12 animals that occupy a territory. The group regularly scent-marks its area and makes use of communal dung heaps in the territory. Males do not respect these boundaries and both male and female will ignore them if food is scarce. Females are dominant. Although sometimes seen during the day, they are primarily nocturnal. Scavengers, but may also hunt in a pack.

Food Eats carrion; sometimes hunts antelope such as impala and springbok.

Breeding 1–4 young are born any time during the year (with a peak in late summer) after a gestation period of ±3 months. ♀ has 1 pair of abdominal mammae.

Mass
♂ 46–79 kg, ♀ 56–80 kg

Shoulder height
±77 cm

Age
±25 years

Vocalisation
Well-known *whoo-hoop* sound. Also chilling 'laughing' sounds.

9–12 cm

Cheetah

Acinonyx jubatus
(Jagluiperd)

Mass
♂ 39–60 kg, ♀ 36–48 kg

Shoulder height
±86 cm

R.W.
Min: 12⅝", Max: 14½"

S.C.I.
Min: E.D., Max: 13½ pnts

Age
±12 years

Vocalisation
High-pitched bird-like call.

Subspecies Only one subspecies occurs in this region:

■ *A.j. jubatus*

Identification Slender, with long legs. Small head with distinct dark stripes ('tear marks') from inside corner of the eyes to the mouth. Round or oval black spots over the entire body.

Differs from other species Leopard: sturdier, shorter legs and rosette-like spots.

Difference between ♂ and ♀ The male is slightly heavier.

Habitat A savannah species found in fairly arid areas, but avoids thickets and riverine forests. Prefers more open woodland and plains because of its hunting methods. The presence of prey is important. Independent of water.

Habits Mainly diurnal: most active at sunrise and sunset; rests in a place with a clear view. Usually seen in pairs or alone. Males like to form groups. Home ranges overlap and although males mark their areas with urine, not all of them demonstrate territorial behaviour. Very fast, and relies on its speed to overtake and catch its prey.

Food Ostriches, impala, springbok and other small antelope, calves of larger antelope, and ground-living birds, such as korhaans and guinea-fowl. Also hares and porcupines.

Breeding 1–5 young are born any time during the year after a gestation period of ±3 months. ♀ has 5–6 pairs of pectoral and abdominal mammae.

54

Leopard

Panthera pardus
(Luiperd)

Subspecies Only one subspecies occurs in the region:

■ *P.p. melanotica*

Identification Well built, with a long tail. Light golden-brown, with black spots and rosettes of 4–6 spots arranged in a circle.

Differs from other species Cheetah: slender build, taller on its legs and with single spots. Characteristic 'tear marks'.

Difference between ♂ and ♀ The male is much larger.

Habitat Very adaptable; occurs even in desert areas. Prefers stony hills, riverine forest, broken country, mountains and thickets. Prey and sufficient shelter such as rocks or bushes are essential. Independent of water.

Habits Solitary, except during mating time. Mainly nocturnal, but to a certain extent also diurnal in undisturbed areas. It marks its territory with urine and a male's territory overlaps with those of some females. A very good tree climber and is able to haul even large prey up a tree – out of reach of scavengers. Has keen senses and is very cunning and dangerous.

Food From mice, dassies and bushpigs to small and medium-sized antelope and calves of larger antelope. Big game, such as kudu, are the exception.

Breeding 2–3 (occasionally up to 6) young are born any time during the year, after a gestation period of ±3 months. ♀ has 2 pairs of abdominal mammae.

Mass
♂ 20–82 kg, ♀ 17–35 kg

Shoulder height
±65 cm

R.W.
Min: 15⅝", Max: 19"

S.C.I.
Min: 14 pnts, Max: 19 pnts

Age
±20 years

Vocalisation
Most common is a hoarse 'cough'. Growls, grumbles and purrs.

7–12 cm

♂

♀

Mass
♂ 180–240 kg, ♀ 120–180 kg

Shoulder height
♂ ±106 cm, ♀ ±91 cm

R.W.
Min: 24", Max: 28¾"

S.C.I.
Min: 23 pnts, Max: 27½ pnts

Age
±20 years

Vocalisation
Well-known repeated *uuuh-humph*, growing gradually shorter and softer.

13 cm

Subspecies None.

Identification Largest cat in the region. Young animals have dark rosettes and spots that fade away as the animal matures. The male usually has a dark mane on its head, neck and shoulders.

Difference between ♂ and ♀ The male is much larger than the female. Female has no mane.

Habitat Widespread in savannah and semidesert areas. Availability of especially medium-sized to large game is an important requirement. Also essential are shade for resting during the day and other shelter for stalking its prey. Independent of water.

Habits The only cats that form prides, each with an average of 12 members. Single nomadic lions are also seen. Mainly nocturnal, but also active during the day, especially at sunrise and sunset. Pride consists of one or more males (one of them dominant), a dominant female, other females and young lions. They occupy a territory, but do not necessarily wander together.

Food Anything from mice to buffalo, and even young elephants; prefers blue wildebeest, impala and zebra. Usually hunts in a group at night.

Breeding 1–4 (occasionally 6) cubs are born any time during the year, after a gestation period of ±3 months. ♀ has 2 pairs of abdominal mammae.

Caracal (Lynx)

Felis caracal
(Rooikat)

Subspecies
▬ *F.c. caracal* (dark, brick red)
▬ *F.c. damarensis* (paler, lighter red)

Identification Well-built cat with large paws. It has characteristic tassels of long darker hair on the tips of its ears.

Difference between ♂ and ♀ The male is usually more heavily built than the female.

Habitat Occurs in a variety of habitats, but absent in forests and deserts. Sufficient shelter is of the utmost importance. Prefers open areas: frequents the open areas around vleis and pans, open woodland or grass plains. Independent of water.

Habits Mainly nocturnal and very seldom seen during the day; if so, early in the morning or late afternoon and on cool, overcast days. Solitary and meet only to mate. Although a good tree climber, it lives and hunts mostly on the ground. Rests during the day. Has the ability to hide itself with very little shelter available.

Food Duiker, steenbok, grysbok, bushbuck ewes, Damara dik-dik, young impala and springbok, lambs of sheep, Cape hare, dassies, squirrels, young monkeys, springhare, moles, mice, mongooses, guinea-fowl and other ground-living birds.

Breeding 2–4 (occasionally 5) young are born October–March after a gestation period of ±2 months. ♀ has 5 pairs of pectoral and abdominal mammae.

Mass
♂ 8.6–20 kg, ♀ 4.2–14.5 kg

Shoulder height
±43 cm

Age
±11 years

Vocalisation
Purrs; young chirp like a bird.

5 cm

Serval

Leptailurus serval
(Tierboskat)

Mass
♂ 8.6–13.5 kg, ♀ 8.6–11.8 kg

Shoulder height
±56 cm

Age
±12 years

Mass
♂ 1.5–1.7 kg, ♀ 1.0–1.4 kg

Vocalisation
Grunts, grumbles and spits.

Subspecies Only one subspecies occurs in this region:
■ *F.s. serval*

Identification Slender, with very long legs and large ears. The black stripes on the neck change into spots stretching in a line from the front backwards.

Difference between ♂ and ♀ The male is slightly heavier than the female.

Habitat Absent in dry areas such as deserts or semideserts. Only enters an arid area when a river provides a suitable habitat. Prefers savannah with high rainfall, or areas containing stagnant water. Water and sufficient shelter, such as thick grass, clumps of bushes or reeds, are important requirements.

Habits Mainly nocturnal and seldom seen during the day. They sometimes hunt in pairs, but are usually solitary. Ranges far in search of food, using footpaths on its way to hunt to avoid difficult terrain. Hunts vlei rats in swampy areas among watergrass, where the water may be up to 8 cm deep. Not an eager tree climber, but will take to the trees when attacked. Fast over short distances.

Food Mainly vlei rats and mice. Also finches, ducks, lizards, snakes, scrub hares, cane rats and locusts. Sometimes returns to prey of the previous day.

Breeding 1–4 young are born September–April after a gestation period of ±2 months. ♀ has 1 pair of groin and 2 pairs of abdominal mammae.

Small spotted cat (Black-footed cat)

Felis nigripes
(Klein gekolde kat)

Subspecies

F.n. nigripes (light yellowish brown, rusty dark brown spots and stripes)

F.n. thomasi (brownish yellow, distinct black spots and stripes)

Identification The smallest cat of the region. Light yellowish brown with dark spots. Has dark stripes against the neck and throat.

Differs from other species African wild cat: larger, tawny-grey colour and without the distinct dark spots on the body.

Difference between ♂ and ♀ The male is slightly more heavily built than the female.

Habitat Only found in more arid areas (100–500 mm/annum). Prefers open areas that offer shelter, such as patches of tall grass or shrubs, to which to flee. Also uses shelters such as springhare or antbear holes or holes in anthills in which to rest during the day. Independent of water.

Habits Nocturnal, appearing only some hours after sunset. Usually solitary, except in the mating season when a few males accompany a female. Lives and hunts mainly on the ground, but is a good tree climber. Rests during the heat of day. Shy and very aggressive for its size.

Food Mainly mice and spiders. Also agamas, ground-living birds and insects.

Breeding 1–3 young are born November–December after a gestation period of ±2 months.

Mass
♂ 1.5–1.7 kg, ♀ 1.0–1.4 kg

Shoulder height
±25 cm

Age
Unknown

Vocalisation
Spits and also growls.

2.5 cm

African wild cat

Felis silvestris lybica
(Vaalboskat)

Mass
♂ 3.8–6.4 kg, ♀ 2.6–5.5 kg

Shoulder height
±35 cm

Age
Unknown

Vocalisation
Groans, hisses, growls and spits.

Subspecies This cat is now a subspecies of the domestic cat *Felis silvestris*.

Identification Resembles a grey domestic cat; has long legs. Tawny-grey with dark stripes and rings on the legs and tail. Reddish behind the ears.

Differs from other species Domestic cat (or crosses between the two): shorter legs, more spots on the body and lacks the reddishness behind the ears. Small spotted cat: smaller and lighter in colour, with distinct spots on the body.

Difference between ♂ and ♀ The male is more heavily built than the female.

Habitat Widespread except in mountain forests and deserts. Requires shelter, such as rocky slopes, dense bush, reeds or tall grass, antbear holes or holes in anthills in which to rest during the day. Independent of water.

Habits Mainly solitary and nocturnal, and appears only after sunset. Although a good tree climber, it lives predominantly on the ground. Territorial, with both male and female marking and defending their area. They like to use the same footpaths. Crossbreeds easily with the domestic cat.

Food Mice, vlei rats, rats, ducks, chickens, doves, bustards, lizards, snakes, hares, springhares, spiders, frogs and wild fruit.

Breeding 2–5 young are born any time of the year after a gestation period of ±2 months.

Rock hyrax (Dassie)

Procavia capensis
(Klipdassie)

Subspecies None.

Identification Small and sturdy, with short legs and no tail. On the back is a patch of black hair.

Differs from other species Yellow-spotted rock hyrax: slightly smaller, patch on the back is yellow and the spots above the eyes are white. Tree hyrax: fur is longer than that of the other two species and the patch on the back is white.

Difference between ♂ and ♀ The male is slightly heavier than the female.

Habitat Rocky area with crevices, caves or holes for shelter, as well as shrubs and/or trees. Usually found on a stony hill, cliff or even small stone heaps where yellow-spotted dassies do not occur.

Habits Gregarious, lives in colonies that could number a few hundred with definite hierarchy. Often lives together with yellow-spotted dassies. Mainly diurnal: forages early in the morning and late in the afternoon – even well into the night if there is sufficient moonlight. On cold mornings, it first warms itself by sitting in the sun, while a female stands sentry. Uses fixed latrine places.

Food Grass, herbs, shrubs and other leaves.

Breeding 1–6 young are born September–October (winter rainfall areas) and March–April (summer rainfall areas) after a gestation period of ±7 months.

Mass
♂ 3.2–4.7 kg, ♀ 2.5–4.2 kg

Shoulder height
±25 cm

Age
±6 years

Vocalisation
Sharp alarm bark, snorts, screams, growls and chirps.

3.5 cm

Black rhinoceros (Hooked-lipped rhinoceros)

Diceros bicornis
(Swartrenoster)

Mass
♂ 730–970 kg, ♀ 760–1 000 kg

Shoulder height
±160 cm

R.W.
Min: 24", Max: 53½"

S.C.I.
Min: 56 pnts, Max: 89¼ pnts

Age
±40 years

Vocalisation
Snorts, screams and growls.
Cows call calves with a 'mewing'
sound.

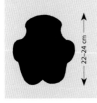

22–24 cm

Subspecies
- *D.b. bicornis* (extinct)
- *D.b. minor*

Identification Huge, with two horns on top of the snout and a pointed prehensile upper lip. Sometimes has bloody skin lesions caused by parasites.

Differs from other species White rhinoceros: larger, with elongated head, a hump on the neck and a square mouth. Walks with its head close to the ground.

Difference between ♂ and ♀ The cow is slightly heavier.

Habitat Woodland with thickets for shelter and water to drink and in which to bathe. Shrubs and trees of up to 4 m are essential for browsing (will even push down trees to reach leaves). Dependent on water; seldom further than 15 km from water.

Habits Solitary. Although the bulls spray urine on bushes and have dung heaps, they are not territorial animals as home ranges overlap. Bulls fight over a cow in oestrus and not over territory. Aggressive and although it avoids contact, serious fights do occur. Rests in shade or wallows in the mud when hot. Calf usually walks behind its mother.

Food Leaves, small branches, sticks and thorns. When available, drinks water daily – usually at night. Sometimes digs in the sand if water has dried up.

Breeding 1 calf is born any time during the year after a gestation period of ±15 months. ♀ has 1 pair of groin mammae.

White rhinoceros (Square-lipped rhinoceros)

Ceratotherium simum
(Witrenoster)

Subspecies Only one subspecies occurs in the region:

■ *C.s. simum*

Identification Huge, with an elongated head and two horns on the snout. Mouth is square and wide.

Differs from other species Black rhinoceros: smaller with a prehensile upper lip and shorter head. Has no hump on the neck. Walks with head held high.

Difference between ♂ and ♀ The bull is heavier than the cow.

Habitat Wooded grass plains with open marshes and enough water. Important requirements include areas with short grass, availability of water to drink as well as in which to bathe, thickets for shelter and fairly flat terrain.

Habits Lives in small groups consisting of a territorial bull, other bulls (tolerated by him), cows and young. A territorial bull sprays urine and defecates in latrines along boundaries as a way of marking its territory. Only the territorial bull urinates by spraying through its hind legs; others urinate normally. The territories of territorial bulls become larger in dry seasons, while the home ranges of cows overlap. Has poor eyesight, but acute senses of hearing and smell. The calf usually walks in front of its mother.

Food Grass, especially short grass. Drinks water when it is available.

Breeding 1 calf is born any time during the year after a gestation period of ±16 months. ♀ has 1 pair of groin mammae.

Mass
♂ 2000–2300 kg,
♀ 1400–1600 kg

Shoulder height
±170 cm

R.W.
Min: 28", Max: 62¼"

S.C.I.
Min: 70 pnts, Max: 95¾ pnts

Age
±45 years

Vocalisation
Pants to keep contact. Blows, snorts, yells and growls.

23–28 cm

Elephant

Loxodonta africana
(Olifant)

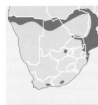

Mass
♂ 5500–6000 kg,
♀ 3600–4000 kg

Shoulder height
±3.5 m

Record tusk length
11'5"

R.W.
Min: 80 lb, Max: 226 lb

S.C.I.
Min: 100 pnts, Max: 228 pnts

Age
±65 years

Vocalisation
Screams and trumpets. Keeps contact by deep rumbling.

52 cm

Subspecies Only one subspecies occurs in the region:
■ *L.a. africana*

Identification A huge animal with long thick legs and very large ears. Its trunk is versatile, acting as nose and hand. Usually has long tusks.

Difference between ♂ and ♀ The bull is larger than the cow and has larger and heavier tusks.

Habitat Found in areas ranging from the arid Kaokoland to dense savannah with a high rainfall. Clear drinking water, other permanent water, shade and enough food (grass and branches) are essential. Dependent on water.

Habits Diurnal and nocturnal. Gregarious: herds consist mainly of a cow and her descendants. Bulls form temporary male herds or live alone (especially the old ones), only joining the cows for mating. Large breeding herds with bulls also exist. It shows aggression when it lifts it trunk and head, spreads out its ears and trumpets, or kicks up dust. When drinking, it squirts water over itself or lies down to cool off. Enjoys wallowing in mud, and rubbing against trees.

Food Branches, grass, leaves, bark and fruit. May drink water once in four days or even daily. Water for drinking must be clear – and it may even dig in the sand.

Breeding 1 (rarely 2) calves are born at any time during the year after a gestation period of ±22 months. ♀ has 1 pair mammae between the front legs.

Hippopotamus

Subspecies

■ *H.a. capensis*

■ *H.a. constrictus*

Identification A very large, barrel-shaped body and short legs. The skin is naked and predominantly greyish-brown, but yellowish-pink against the throat, belly and some skin folds.

Difference between ♂ and ♀ The male is larger.

Habitat Open stretches of permanent water or riverine pools with gently sloping sandbanks on which to rest. The area should contain enough food. Prefers pools that are deep enough for submersion, with slow-running water. Moves away during floods, but returns to the same pools if they have not changed much.

Habits Grazes at night. Rests during the day, half-submerged or on a sandbank if it is not too hot. Sometimes grazes far from water, especially during dry periods. Makes use of the same route frequently and leaves a double-track game path. Gregarious, with herds consisting of 10–15 animals. If pools with sufficient water become scarce towards the end of winter, larger numbers of animals congregate together. Although an adult male leads the group to grazing areas at night, there is a definite hierarchy with a cow as the leader.

Food Grass (130 kg in order to be satiated).

Breeding 1 young is born any time during the year after a gestation period of 7–8 months. ♀ has 1 pair groin mammae.

Mass
♂ 970–2000 kg, ♀ 995–1675 kg

Shoulder height
♂ ±150 cm, ♀ ±144 cm

R.W.
Min: 29¾", Max: 64½"

S.C.I.
Min: 50 pnts, Max: 88⅜ pnts

Age
±39 years

Vocalisation
High-pitched roaring bellow followed by 5 short ones at a lower pitch.

← 22–25 cm →

Antbear (Aardvark)

Orycteropus afer
(Erdvark)

Mass
♂ 41–65 kg, ♀ 40–58 kg

Shoulder height
±61 cm

Age
±10 years

Vocalisation
Grunts and snuffles, otherwise silent.

Subspecies Only one subspecies occurs in the region:
■ *O.a. afer*

Identification The hindquarters are much heavier than the forequarters. Has an elongated, pig-like snout, long ears and a thick, tapering tail.

Difference between ♂ and ♀ The male is slightly heavier than the female.

Habitat Prefers open woodland (dry islands in the Okavango swamps), grassland or shrubby areas. Although it seems to prefer sandy soil, it is also found on more clayish soil such as that found in mopane veld. The availability of termites is a determinant. Independent of water.

Habits Solitary and mainly nocturnal: sleeps during the day in a hole, after it has closed the entrance; only appears late at night. Travels long distances in search of food, with its nose held close to the ground. Acute senses of smell and hearing, but poor eyesight. There are three types of holes: permanent burrows with several tunnels and entrances, semipermanent shelters, and diggings made in search of food that are not used again. The tongue is very sticky and is used to catch termites and ants.

Food Mainly termites and ants.

Breeding 1 young is born July–September after a gestation period of ±7 months.

Giraffe

Giraffe camelopardalis
(Kameelperd)

Subspecies

■ *G.c. capensis*
■ *G.c. angolensis*

Identification Unmistakable long neck and legs. Light brown patches on yellowish to white background. Two short horns on the head.

Difference between ♂ and ♀ The male is usually heavier than the female.

Habitat Occurs in a variety of plant habitats. Found in dry woodland, from low shrubveld to fairly dense woodland. An important requirement is the presence of the different plants (especially thorn trees) on which it feeds throughout the year. Avoids very dense bush. Independent of water.

Habits Mainly diurnal. Rests standing or lying down during the heat of the day, with its head held upright. Sleeps with the head bending backwards against the body. Gregarious with loose associations; individuals wander between herds. Herds consist of females and their young, but there are also herds consisting of males, females and young. Although most adult males go single, younger males form male herds that have a hierarchy. Males fight using their heads.

Food Mainly leaves, especially of thorn trees in the wet season and of evergreen trees in the dry season. Drinks water regularly when available.

Breeding 1 young is born any time during the year after a gestation period of ±15 months. ♀ has 2 pairs of groin mammae.

Mass
♀ 970–1395 kg, ♀ 700–950 kg

Shoulder height
±300 cm

Age
±28 years

Vocalisation
Snorts or grunts when alarmed, bellows when hungry.

19–21 cm

Bushpig

Potamochoerus porcus
(Bosvark)

Mass
♂ 46–82 kg, ♀ 48–66 kg

Shoulder height
±75 cm

R.W.
Min: 5½", Max: 11⅞"

S.C.I.
Min: 11 pnts, Max: 22¼ pnts

Age
±20 years

Vocalisation
Groans while eating. Alarm call is a long, protracted growl.

Subspecies

▤ *P.p. nyasae*

■ *P.p. koiropotamus*

Identification Resembles the domestic pig. Predominantly brown, with a mane of lighter hair. The young have horizontal white stripes on their bodies.

Differs from other species Warthog: greyer, with larger canine teeth, a broad snout and warts on the face.

Difference between ♂ and ♀ The male is usually heavier.

Habitat Thick shelter and water are essential. Prefers coastal, mountainous and riverine forests, thickets, reed patches and tall grass near water. Found only under these conditions even in dry country.

Habits Lives in groups of 7 animals (even up to 12), consisting of a dominant male, dominant female, other females and young. Groups with young are very aggressive. Mainly nocturnal, but also diurnal in areas where it is protected. Forages at night, tramping out footpaths. Digs in the soil like warthogs, and likes to wallow in mud to cool down.

Food Digs in soft soil for rhizomes, bulbs and tubers. Also eats earthworms, vegetables, chickens, leaves and wild fruit that have fallen.

Breeding 3–8 young are born November–January after a gestation period of ±4 months. ♀ has 3 pairs of abdominal mammae.

Common warthog

Phacochoerus aethiopicus
(Vlakvark)

♂   ♀

Subspecies

▓ *P.a. aethiopicus*
▓ *P.a. sundevalli*
▤ *P.a. shortridgei*

Identification The snout is broader than that of a domestic pig and long canine teeth curl over the snout. Lifts its tail vertically when it runs away.

Differs from other species Bushpig: brown; lighter mane, narrower snout, smaller canine teeth and usually no warts.

Difference between ♂ and ♀ Male has two pairs of warts; female only 1 pair. Male is much larger, with longer canines.

Habitat Areas with short grass and mud pools. Prefers open woodland, grass plains (especially floodplains), vleis and open areas surrounding pans and water holes. Likes areas where fresh grass grows following a fire. Avoids thickets. Independent of water.

Habits Lives in family groups (male, female and her young) nursing groups (one or more females and their young) and temporary male groups, but solitary males are not uncommon. Diurnal and sleeps at night in old antbear holes, which it enters backwards. Such holes also serve as a shelter against predators and bad weather. Home ranges overlap and become larger in dry seasons. Likes to wallow in mud.

Food Grass, rhizomes and fruit. Drinks water when available.

Breeding 1–8 young are born September–December after a gestation period of ±5 months. ♀ has 2 pairs of groin mammae.

Mass
♂ 60–100 kg, ♀ 45–70 kg

Shoulder height
±60 cm

R.W.
Min: 13", Max: 24"

S.C.I.
Min: 30 pnts, Max: 49⅞ pnts

Age
±20 years

Vocalisation
Growls, snorts and grunts. The male snaps its jaws as an overture to mating.

5.5 cm

Plains zebra

Equus quagga
(Vlaktekwagga)

Mass
♂ 290–340 kg, ♀ 290–325 kg

Shoulder height
±134 cm

Age
±35 years

Vocalisation
A *qua-ha-ha* whinny, followed by a whistling sound when air is inhaled; this is repeated a few times.

Subspecies It has been determined that the plains zebra is now the same species as the `extinct' quagga, which means that the zebra previously known as the Burchell's zebra is a subspecies of the quagga and so the quagga species was never really extinct.

Identification Horse-like animals, with stripes on the flanks that continue onto the belly. Dull shadow stripes on the white stripes. Lower down near the hooves stripes become indistinct.

Differs from other species Mountain zebra: it has a dewlap, legs are striped to the hooves, the belly is white and it does not have the shadow stripes.

Difference between ♂ and ♀ Stallion slightly heavier than the mare.

Habitat A savannah species: prefers open woodland, grassland and floodplains. Avoids dense savannah and is seldom seen further than 12 km from water. Ranges in search of grazing areas, but availability of water is the determinant.

Habits Gregarious: forms herds consisting of a stallion, one or more mares and their offspring. Other stallions form male herds or go on their own. Fond of dust baths. In some areas, move over large distances from winter- to summer-grazing areas, leaving the summer-grazing area just before the seasonal water supply dries up.

Food Mainly grass, but sometimes leaves, branches and pods. Drinks water regularly.

Breeding 1 foal is born any time during the year (peaking in summer) after a gestation period of ±12 months. ♀ has 1 pair of groin mammae.

Mountain zebra

Equus zebra
(Bergkwagga)

Cape mountain zebra

Hartmann's mountain zebra

Subspecies

E.z. zebra (broader stripes on buttocks)

E.z. hartmannae (larger, narrower stripes on buttocks)

Identification Horse-like, with a dewlap and black stripes that end on the flanks – leaving the belly white – but extending down the legs to the hooves.

Differs from other species Plains zebra: without dewlap, stripes continue onto the belly; there are also shadow stripes on the white stripes.

Difference between ♂ and ♀ The male is slightly larger than the female.

Habitat Restricted to mountainous areas containing their preferential grazing, water and ravines for shelter against cold winds. Prefers plateaus and mountain slopes. *E.z. hartmannae* moves seasonally downhill for grazing. Dependent on water.

Habits Diurnal: active during the cooler parts of the day and rests when it is warm. Gregarious, with herds consisting mainly of a dominant stallion, mares and foals. Mares usually spend their whole lives in the same herd. Some stallions move on their own while others form male herds. From time to time, younger stallions challenge the dominant stallions in the breeding herd to depose them.

Food Mainly grass, but occasionally also shrubs and twigs. Drinks water regularly (at least once a day).

Breeding 1 foal is born any time during the year after a gestation period of ±12 months. ♀ has 1 pair of groin mammae.

Mass
♂ 250–330 kg, ♀ 204–300 kg

Shoulder height
±126–150 cm

Age
±35 years

Vocalisation
Snorts and a shrill alarm call.

11 cm

Blue wildebeest (Brindled gnu)

Connochaetes taurinus
(Blouwildebees)

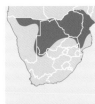

Mass
♂ 230–270 kg, ♀ 160–200 kg

Shoulder height
♂ ±150 cm, ♀ ±135 cm

R.W.
Min: 28½", Max: 33⅛"

S.C.I.
Min: 70 pnts, Max: 94¾ pnts

Age
±20 years

Vocalisation
Snorts, bellows and grunts.
Calves bleat; young ones make a
humm sound.

9.5–11 cm

Subspecies Only one subspecies occurs in the region:
◼ *C.t. taurinus*

Identification Cattle-like, with the face, mane and horse's tail black. Dark vertical stripes on the neck and flanks. Both males and females have horns.

Differs from other species Black wildebeest: smaller with horns curving forward and upwards and a white tail. Absent in savannah.

Difference between ♂ and ♀ The male is larger than the female.

Habitat Open savannah, especially thorn and tamboti woodland. Prefers short grass plains in valleys and floodplains. Seasonal movements take place to areas with short grass if the grass in the particular area becomes too tall and the number of parasites increases. Dependent on water.

Habits Usually forms herds of 20–30 animals. There are female and bachelor herds as well as territorial males with female herds forming the closest association. Female herds may move through a male's territory. Bachelor herds have a loose association. Grazes when it is cool and rests in the shade during the hottest part of the day. Settled in certain areas, but migrates seasonally to other areas, forming larger herds numbering thousands.

Food Mainly short grass of up to 15 cm. Sometimes also bark and leaves.

Breeding 1 (occasionally 2) young are born November–February after a gestation period of ±8 months. ♀ has 1 pair of groin mammae.

72

Black wildebeest (White-tailed gnu)

Connochaetes gnou
(Swartwildebees)

Subspecies None.

Identification Cattle-like, appears to be sulky, characteristic beard and hair on the nose. Distinctive long, almost white horse's tail. Both male and female have horns.

Differs from other species Blue wildebeest: larger, with the horns bent sideways, and a black tail. Not found in the Highveld.

Difference between ♂ and ♀ The male is larger than the female.

Habitat Found in open plains with water; grass plains of the Free State and Highveld. In the past, occurred in abundance in the Karoo areas of the Northern Cape. Dependent on water.

Habits Gregarious; female herds, bachelor herds and territorial males can be distinguished. A territorial male is closely attached to its territory throughout the year, marking it with urine and glandular excretions; it is the only male in the herd that mates. Female herds are allowed to pass freely through his territory. Threatening behaviour: pawing or horning the ground and kneeling; serious fights are rare. Herds are active early in the morning and late in the afternoon. They rest during the heat of the day and these resting periods become shorter during winter.

Food Grass, also Karoo bushes. Drinks water regularly, mainly in the late afternoons.

Breeding 1 young is born December–January after a gestation period of ±8 months. ♀ has 1 pair groin mammae.

Mass
♂ ±180 kg, ♀ ±140 kg

Shoulder height
♂ ±120 cm, ♀ ±110 cm

R.W.
Min: 22¼", Max: 29⅜"

S.C.I.
Min: 72 pnts, Max: 95½ pnts

Age
±20 years

Vocalisation
Snorts and a loud *ghe-nu* sound by territorial males.

7.5–9.5 cm

Bontebok / Blesbok

Damaliscus pygargus
(Bontebok / Blesbok)

Bontebok

Blesbok

Mass
♂ ±64/70 kg, ♀ ±59/61 kg

Shoulder height
±90/95 cm

R.W.
Min: 14/16½", Max: 16¾/20⅜"

S.C.I.
Min: 36/39 pnts,
Max: 47½/58¼ pnts

Age
±11 years

Vocalisation
Snorts and also growls.

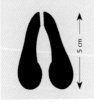

Subspecies

▇ *D.p. dorcas* (larger white patches, especially on the croup)

▇ *D.p. phillipsi* (smaller white patches; the small and large blaze on the face are usually divided)

Identification Distinct white blaze on the face. The belly, inner parts of the buttocks and the legs below the knee are white. Both male and female have horns.

Difference between ♂ and ♀ The male is slightly larger than the female and its horns are thicker.

Habitat Grass plains with sufficient drinking water and cover. Blesbok prefers sweet grass plains. Bontebok lives in a coastal plain in the Cape fynbos area that contains plenty of grass and shrubs for cover.

Habits Diurnal: grazes in early morning and late afternoon, resting in the shade when hot. Walks in single file between drinking and feeding places. Gregarious: territorial males, female herds and bachelor herds can be distinguised. Territories are maintained by challenging displays, threatening behaviour and marking of grass with preorbital glands. Territorial males make use of common dung heaps and sometimes lie down on top of them to rest. The blesbok's territorial behaviour becomes less marked and herd structures change after the mating season, while those of the bontebok remain unchanged.

Food Grass, especially short or in burnt areas. Drinks water regularly.

Breeding 1 young is born September–November (bontebok) and November–January (blesbok) after a gestation period of ±8 months. ♀ has 1 pair of groin mammae.

Tsessebe (Sassaby)

Damaliscus lunatus
(Basterhartbees)

Subspecies Only one subspecies occurs in the region:

▪ *D.l. lunatus*

Identification Dark reddish-brown with a metallic sheen. The blaze on the face, buttocks, shoulders and upper legs is black. Both males and females have horns.

Differs from other species Red hartebeest: a redder colour; horns are closer at the base. Lichtenstein's hartebeest: yellowish-brown, without black on blaze and upper legs.

Difference between ♂ and ♀ The male is heavier than the female.

Habitat Prefers open areas on the edge of grass plains with woodland. Medium to tall tasty grass, shade and water are important requirements. Makes temporary use of areas with only seasonal water.

Habits Fastest antelope of the region. Gregarious; forms herds of 2–30, while larger herds are also known. There are territorial males, breeding herds and bachelor herds. A territorial male regularly patrols its borders, marking them with droppings and manoeuvering the grass stems into its preorbital glands. Enjoys horning the ground. In mating season, a male gathers a harem in his area, taking over the leadership and expelling the young males in the herd.

Food Grass. Drinks water regularly.

Breeding 1 young is born September–November after a gestation period of ±8 months. ♀ has 1 pair of groin mammae.

Mass
♂ 140 kg, ♀ 126 kg

Shoulder height
♂ ±126 cm, ♀ ±125 cm

R.W.
Min: 15", Max: 18½"

S.C.I.
Min: 40 pnts, Max: 58¾ pnts

Age
±15 years

Vocalisation
Snorts.

6–9 cm

Red hartebeest (Cape hartebeest)

Alcelaphus buselaphus
(Rooihartbees)

Mass
♂ 137–180 kg, ♀ 105–136 kg

Shoulder height
♂ ±125 cm, ♀ ±119 cm

R.W.
Min: 23", Max: 29½"

S.C.I.
Min: 62 pnts, Max: 80¼ pnts

Age
±13 years

Vocalisation
Sneezing-snorting sound
as an alarm.

8.5–12 cm

Subspecies Only one subspecies occurs in the region:

■ *A.b. caama*

Identification Glossy reddish-brown. The tail, blaze on the face and the outside of the legs are black. Both males and females have horns.

Differs from other species Lichtenstein's hartebeest: lighter in colour; shins are black and the horns further apart at the base. Tsessebe: horns are different and the black against the legs extends further up.

Difference between ♂ and ♀ The male is larger than the female.

Habitat Found in semidesert savannah. May occur in open woodland, but avoids dense woodland. Prefers open plains such as grass plains, floodplains, grassland, vleis and the strips of grass around pans. Independent of water.

Habits Gregarious: forms herds of up to 20 animals. Mass herds of thousands have been seen in Botswana. Territorial males, harem herds, bachelor herds and solitary males exist. Harem herds are stable and consist of a territorial male as the leader, young males, females and their offspring. Active in the early mornings and late afternoons; lies in the sun to rest, except when it is very hot.

Food Grass (especially red-grass), and also leaves. Drinks when water is available.

Breeding 1 young is born October–December after a gestation period of ±8 months. ♀ has 1 pair of groin mammae.

Lichtenstein's hartebeest

Alcelaphus lichtensteinii
(Mofhartbees)

Subspecies None.

Identification The shins and the tuft of long hair on the tail are black. The dark patch behind the shoulders is caused by the animal rubbing its horns and face there after horning the ground. Both males and females have horns.

Differs from other species Red hartebeest: darker reddish-brown. The upper legs and the blaze on the face are black. Tsessebe: darker with black blaze and legs. Horns wider.

Difference between ♂ and ♀ The male is slightly larger than the female.

Habitat A savannah species. Prefers the strips of grassveld between vleis (or floodplains) and the surrounding woodland that contain enough water and sufficient perennial types of grass. Dependent on water.

Habits Gregarious; herds of 3–12 animals consisting of a territorial male, some females and their offspring. Other males either go single or form herds. The territorial male keeps a distance from his females and watches the vicinity from high positions such as anthills. He marks his territory by creating latrines and by rubbing the preorbital glands on the ground. Acute sense of sight, but poor sense of smell.

Food Mainly grass, especially fresh sprouts. Drinks water regularly.

Breeding A single young is born June–September after a gestation period of ±8 months. ♀ has 1 pair of groin mammae.

Mass
♂ 157–204 kg, ♀ 160–181 kg

Shoulder height
♂ ±129 cm, ♀ ±124 cm

R.W.
Min: 18½", Max: 24⅜"

S.C.I.
Min: 53 pnts, Max: 75¾ pnts

Age
Unknown

Vocalisation
Bellows or a sneezing-snort when alarmed.

8–10 cm

Blue duiker

Cephalophus monticola
(Blouduiker)

Mass
♂ 3.8–5.5 kg, ♀ 4.6–7.3 kg

Shoulder height
♂ ±30 cm, ♀ ±31.5 cm

R.W.
Min: 1¾", Max: 2⅞"

S.C.I.
Min: 4 pnts, Max: 8½ pnts

Age
±7 years

Vocalisation
A piercing alarm whistle. Loud
cat-like 'mew' when in danger.

Subspecies
≡ *C.m. monticola* (dark brown body, tail white underneath)
▬ *C.m. bicolor* (upper parts reddish-brown)
▬ *C.m. hecki* (upper parts rust brown, neck greyish-brown)

Identification The smallest antelope of the region. Greyish-brown with a slight blueish sheen on its back. The throat, chest and belly are a lighter colour, almost white. Both males and females have horns.

Differs from other species Red duiker: larger, more reddish.

Difference between ♂ and ♀ The female is slightly larger than the male.

Habitat Limited to very dense coastal and other forests. Although it feeds in the more open areas in the forest, it requires patches of dense undergrowth so that it can flee or rest during the day. Dependent on water.

Habits Solitary. Forages in more open areas and even at the edge of the forest in the early morning and from late afternoon until about 22:00. Very shy and flees to dense undergrowth at the slightest sign of danger. Always alert when nearing an open patch in the forest; it hesitates, making very sure there is no danger before going further. Tramps definite footpaths in the forest between resting places and foraging or drinking places.

Food Leaves, wild fruit (dropped by monkeys) and small branches. Drinks water regularly.

Breeding 1 young is born any time during the year after a gestation period of ±4 months. ♀ has 2 pairs of groin mammae.

Red duiker

Subspecies

█ *C.n. natalensis* (upper parts dark orange-red, and underparts lighter)

█ *C.n. robertsi* (upper parts more orange, and underparts lighter)

Identification A distinct deep chestnut-red. A tuft of long darker hair between the horns. Both male and female have horns.

Differs from other species Blue duiker: smaller and greyish-brown in colour.

Difference between ♂ and ♀ None.

Habitat Confined to thickets and forests with well-developed undergrowth. Dependent on water. Limited to dense mountainous forest, riverine forest, wooded ravines and coastal forest with water.

Habits Solitary, although pairs or a female with her young are also seen. Very timid and is seldom seen except on cool, cloudy days. Takes flight to denser areas at the slightest sign of danger. Likes to forage beneath trees where samango monkeys have dropped fruit. Uses communal dung heaps. May be territorial.

Food Fresh and dry leaves, small branches and wild fruit. Drinks water regularly.

Breeding 1 young is born any time during the year after an uncertain gestation period (probably about 160–167 days). ♀ has 2 pairs of groin mammae.

Mass
11–14 kg

Shoulder height
±43 cm

R.W.
Min: 2½", Max: 4⅛"

S.C.I.
Min: 8 pnts, Max: 13⅜ pnts

Age
±12 years

Vocalisation
A loud *chee-chee* sound (louder than that of a suni) and a whistling, screaming sound.

2,5 cm

Grey duiker (Common duiker)

Sylvicapra grimmia
(Duiker)

♂

♀

Subspecies
- S.g. grimmia
- S.g. caffra
- S.g. orbicularis
- S.g. burchelli
- S.g. steinhardti
- S.g. splendidula

Identification A black stripe on the snout from the forehead to the nose.

Differs from other species Red duiker: somewhat smaller and more reddish.

Difference between ♂ and ♀ Female slightly larger; only the male has horns.

Habitat Prefers woodland with sufficient undergrowth and thickets. Important requirements are thickets, shrubs or tall grass on which it feeds, and in which it takes shelter when in danger and to rest. Avoids open woodland, short grassland and dense mountain or coastal forests. Independent of water.

Habits Solitary, except in the mating season. Forages in the early mornings and late afternoons until after dark. Active for longer periods on cool, cloudy days. More nocturnal outside conservation areas. Lies down to rest in dense shelter, underneath shrubs or in tall grass during the hottest part of the day. Waits until the last moment before running away, head down and with characteristic jumping and swerving movements. Acute senses of smell and sight.

Food Leaves, small branches, fruit, flowers, seed and vegetables. Seldom drinks.

Breeding 1 (seldom 2) young are born any time during the year after a gestation period of ±3 months. ♀ has 2 pairs of groin mammae.

Mass
♂ 15–21 kg, ♀ 17–25 kg

Shoulder height
♂ ±50 cm, ♀ ±52 cm

R.W.
Min: 4½", Max: 7⅞"

S.C.I.
Min: 11 pnts, Max: 19⅜ pnts

Age
±10 years

Vocalisation
A nasal snort as an alarm call. Loud scream when in danger.

3 cm

Suni (Livingstone's antelope)

Neotragus moschatus
(Soenie)

♂ *N.m. zuluensis*

♀ *N.m. zuluensis*

Subspecies

▬ *N.m. livingstonianus*
▬ *N.m. zuluensis*

Identification One of our smallest antelope. The tail is long and dark, and has a white edge. The upper lip protrudes over the lower lip.

Differs from other species Red duiker: larger and more reddish; horns are closer together, the tail is shorter and not as dark.

Difference between ♂ and ♀ Female has no horns, and is heavier than the male.

Habitat Prefers dry savannah with sufficient undergrowth and scrub for cover, as well as riverine forest and dry bush along tributaries. Also found in deciduous woodland with thick undergrowth. Independent of water.

Habits Occur solitary, in pairs or family groups. Diurnal: grazes in the early mornings and late afternoons (for longer periods in cooler weather). Rests during the hottest part of the day. Shy and is seldom seen. When disturbed, it stands dead still for a while before running off, making a *chee-chee* sound. Uses communal dung heaps and has small home ranges (may be territorial). Uses footpaths in dense bush and is easily caught in traps.

Food Leaves and wild fruit. Does not drink water.

Breeding 1 young is born August–February after a gestation period of ±4 months. ♀ has 2 pairs of groin mammae.

Mass
♂ 4.5–5.2 kg, ♀ 5.1–6.8 kg

Shoulder height
±35 cm

R.W.
Min: 3", Max: 5¼"

S.C.I.
Min: 9 pnts, Max: 11¼ pnts

Age
Unknown

Vocalisation
Snorts and makes a high-pitched *chee-chee* whistling sound (softer than that of the red duiker).

2 cm

Klipspringer

Oreotragus oreotragus
(Klipspringer)

♂   ♀

Mass
♂ 9–12 kg, ♀ 11–16 kg

Shoulder height
±58 cm

R.W.
Min: 4⅛", Max: 6¼"

S.C.I.
Min: 11 pnts, Max: 16¼ pnts

Age
±7 years

Vocalisation
A loud, high-pitched explosion of air when alarmed.

Subspecies

 O.o. oreotragus   ▬ *O.o. transvalensis*
▬ *O.o. tyleri*   ▬ *O.o. stevensoni*
▬ *O.o. centralis*

Identification The black speckles on brownish background provide good camouflage when in their rocky habitat. Large black 'tear marks' in the inner corners of the eyes.

Differs from other species Common duiker: slightly heavier, lacks the distinct black speckles on the coat and the black 'tear marks' in the corner of the eyes.

Difference between ♂ and ♀ The female is heavier than the male, but does not have horns.

Habitat Associated with rocky areas: mountains with rocks bordering ravines, ridges with rocks and juts, and rocky hills. Wanders over long distances. Independent of water.

Habits Occur mostly in pairs, but occasionally in family groups or single. Males establish their territories by forming dung heaps and scent-marking them with preorbital glands. Feeds in the early morning and late afternoon, even after dark, and rests in the shade in their rocky habitat. A very sure-footed rock climber, closely confined to the rocky habitat. If disturbed while grazing on the surrounding flats, it immediately takes to rocky shelters.

Food Mainly leaves, and occasionally grass. Drinks water when available.

Breeding 1 young is born any time during the year after a gestation period of 7–7½ months. ♀ has 2 pairs of groin mammae.

Damara dik-dik

Madoqua kirkii
(Damara dik-dik)

♂   ♀

Subspecies Only one subspecies occurs in the region:

■ *M.k. damarensis*

Identification A very small antelope, with an elongated snout and white around the eyes. On top of the forehead is a tuft of long hair.

Differs from other species Steenbok: larger, of lighter colour and the horns are vertical.

Difference between ♂ and ♀ Only the male has horns.

Habitat Thickets and dense woodland on hard, stony ground with sufficient shrubs and little or no grass. Also found against mountain slopes and in riverine forest along which it can penetrate deep into deserts. Independent of water.

Habits Single, in pairs or in family groups of 3–6 during the dry season. The male probably establishes a territory in mating season. Feeds in the very early mornings and late in the afternoons, even after dark. Rests during the hottest part of the day under thick cover. Uses the communal dung heap in a specific way: first smelling it and scratching together a small heap on which it urinates before it defecates. The female does the same, but does not scratch.

Food Mainly leaves, occasionally green grass. Drinks when water is available.

Breeding 1 young is born December–April after a gestation period of 5–6 months. ♀ has 2 pairs of groin mammae.

Mass
4.3–5.5 kg

Shoulder height
±39 cm

R.W.
Min: 2⅜", Max: 4½"

S.C.I.
Min: 7 pnts, Max: 11¼ pnts

Age
±9 years

Vocalisation
An explosive whistling and a high, trembling, whistling sound.

Oribi

Ourebia ourebi
(Oorbietjie)

♂

♀

Mass
♂ 11–17 kg, ♀ 8–20 kg

Shoulder height
♂ ±58 cm, ♀ ±59 cm

R.W.
Min: 5⅞", Max: 7½"

S.C.I.
Min: 13 pnts, Max: 19½ pnts

Age
±13 years

Vocalisation
A snorting whistle as an
alarm call.

3.5 cm

Subspecies
■ *O.o. ourebi*
■ *O.o. hastata*
■ *O.o. rutila*

Identification A small antelope, with a rust-brown colour. Top part of the tail is black; black spots below the ears.

Differs from other species Steenbok: slightly smaller, without long slender neck, black tail and spots below ears.

Difference between ♂ and ♀ The female is heavier than the male and does not have horns.

Habitat Open grassland or floodplains in well-watered areas, with or without scattered trees and shrubs. Found especially in areas with short grass and isolated patches of tall grass for shelter. Avoids large stretches of tall grass, woodland and dense bush.

Habits Mainly solitary, but occasionally in pairs or small groups. The male is territorial and maintains this for the mating season through ostentation and by marking the grass with preorbital glands. Grazes when it is cool and rests in tall grass. Runs away, prancing and leaping high if disturbed, but is very inquisitive and returns later. The male uses communal dung heaps, but this does not have any territorial function.

Food Mainly grass, sometimes small branches. Does not drink water.

Breeding 1 young born October–December after a gestation period of ±7 months. ♀ has 2 pairs of groin mammae.

Steenbok

Raphicerus campestris
(Steenbok)

♂   ♀

Subspecies

- ▦ *R.c. campestris*
- ▦ *R.c. natalensis*
- ▦ *R.c. steinhardti*
- ▦ *R.c. fulvorubescens*
- ▦ *R.c. capricornis*

Identification A small antelope with large ears. The insides of the ears are white with black stripes. There is a black stripe on top of the muzzle.

Differs from other species Oribi: larger with a longer neck, a black tail and spots below the ears. Grysbok: white speckles on the body and longer hair.

Difference between ♂ and ♀ Only the male has horns.

Habitat Open grassland with patches of tall grass or scattered bushes for shelter. Also in open woodland with bare patches and areas with fresh grass sprouting after a fire. Avoids mountainous areas and grass plains with short grass.

Habits Single or in pairs. Establishes territories that both the male and female defend by displays. There are preferential grazing and resting areas as well as latrines close to the borders of such an area, which are scent-marked with the preorbital, pedal and throat glands. Grazes during the cooler hours of the day and rests in tall grass or beneath a bush when it is hot. Swift-footed, lies waiting until danger is almost upon it before jumping up and running away.

Food Leaves and grass, especially herbs. Seldom drinks.

Breeding 1 (occasionally 2) young are born any time during the year (possibly peaking November–December) after a gestation period of ±6 months. ♀ has 2 pairs of groin mammae.

Mass
♂ 9–13 kg, ♀ 11–13 kg

Shoulder height
±52 cm

R.W.
Min: 4½", Max: 7½"

S.C.I.
Min: 11 pnts, Max: 14¼ pnts

Age
±6 years

Vocalisation
Bleats softly.

3 cm

Cape grysbok

Raphicerus melanotis
(Kaapse grysbok)

♂

♀

Mass
9–12 kg

Shoulder height
±54 cm

R.W.
Min: 3", Max: 5¼"

S.C.I.
Min: 7 pnts, Max: 13 pnts

Age
Unknown

Vocalisation
Unknown

2.5 cm

Subspecies None.

Identification A small antelope with large ears. The colour of the body is dark reddish-brown with white speckles. The face, legs and neck do not have speckles.

Differs from other species Steenbok: does not have white speckles on the body, and prefers more open areas. Sharpe's grysbok: Slightly smaller and of lighter colour.

Difference between ♂ and ♀ Only the male has horns.

Habitat Prefers dense scrub along rivers, at the foot of mountains, ravines, broken country and even coastal forest. Occurs in arid areas containing succulents; sufficient shelter, such as patches with dense shrubs, is essential. Independent of water.

Habits Solitary or in pairs. Mainly nocturnal, but may graze in the later afternoon and rests in thick shelter during the hottest parts of the day. Always vigilant when moving about, lying down at the slightest sign of danger. Remains in this position until the last moment before leaping up and running away.

Food Mainly grass, but also leaves, young vine-shoots and wild fruit. Can go without water for a long period.

Breeding 1 young is born September–October after a gestation period of ±6 months. ♀ has 2 pairs of groin mammae.

Sharpe's grysbok

Raphicerus sharpei
(Tropiese grysbok)

♂

♀

Subspecies Only one subspecies occurs in the region:
■ *R.s. sharpei*

Identification A small antelope, with light reddish-brown body and white speckles. The head, neck and legs do not have speckles and there is a black stripe on the muzzle.

Differs from other species Steenbok: no white speckles, and prefers a more open habitat. Cape grysbok: slightly larger and of darker colour.

Difference between ♂ and ♀ Only the male has horns, and the female is slightly larger than the male.

Habitat Areas with thick undergrowth of shrubs and/or grass of up to 50 cm high. Sometimes also found in rocky areas, but very fond of riverine flora and scrub surrounding koppies. Avoids areas with stretches of tall grass. Independent of water.

Habits Solitary or in pairs. Mainly nocturnal, but may be seen in the early mornings and especially late afternoons. Active for longer periods on cool, overcast days. Rests during the hottest hours of the day beneath a bush or other thick cover. Vigilant and timid; runs away with the body close to the ground.

Food Mainly leaves, but also grass, young sprouts, roots and wild fruit.

Breeding 1 young is born any time during the year after a gestation period of ±7 months. ♀ has 2 pairs of groin mammae.

Mass
6.4–11.3 kg

Shoulder height
45–50 cm

R.W.
Min: 1⅞", Max: 4⅛"

S.C.I.
Min: 5 pnts, Max: 9¾ pnts

Age
Unknown

Vocalisation
Unknown

2.5 cm

Springbok

♂   ♀

Mass
♂ 33–48 kg, ♀ 30–44 kg

Shoulder height
±75 cm

R.W.
Min: 14″, Max: 19¾″

S.C.I.
Min: 30 pnts, Max: 45½ pnts

Age
±10 years

Vocalisation
Low-pitched grumbling bellow.
Whistling snort when upset.

4.5 cm

Subspecies
A.m. marsupialis
A.m. hofmeyri

Identification A distinct dark-brown band on each flank above the white belly. A white face with dark stripes from the eyes to the mouth. Both males and females have horns.

Differs from other species Impala: larger, more reddish-brown, black stripes on the buttocks and tail, and without the black band on the flanks.

Difference between ♂ and ♀ The male is slightly heavier.

Habitat Prefers dry open grass- en shrubveld and dry riverbeds. Important requirements are sufficient plants on which to feed, and bushes that are not too high and dense that block their movements and view. Avoids mountains, woodland and tall grass.

Habits Gregarious: usually form small herds. There are mixed herds, bachelor herds and territorial males. Mixed herds split into nursing herds and new bachelor herds during the lambing season. Territories are maintained by showing-off displays and marking with dung heaps, but are not occupied all year. Grazes in the early morning and late afternoon. 'Pronks' (stotting behaviour) when chased.

Food Grass, sprouts and leaves of Karoo bushes and other herbs. Subsists without water, but drinks even stagnant water when available.

Breeding 1 young is born any time during the year, peaking in the rainy season after a gestation period of ±6 months. ♀ has 1 (sometimes 2) pair/s of groin mammae.

Impala

Aepyceros melampus
(Rooibok)

♂ Black-faced impala   ♀

Subspecies

■ *A.m. melampus* (reddish-brown, no black blaze on face)
■ *A.m. petersi* (dull brown, purple sheen; black blaze and stripes at eyes – black-faced impala)

Identification Athletically built, medium-sized antelope, with characteristic black bands on the tail and buttocks. Patches of black hair occur above ankles.

Differs from other species Reedbuck: greyish-brown with a yellow sheen. Puku: golden-brown. Both lack the black bands on the buttocks and tail.

Difference between ♂ and ♀ The female is smaller and has no horns.

Habitat Open woodland with sufficient water, especially thorn- and mopaneveld; also found in more dense woodland such as that along rivers (especially the black-faced impala) and on the edge of woodland and grassland or floodplains. Dependent on water.

Habits Gregarious: usually forms herds of 6–20 and even more than 100 in winter. Territorial males (only in mating season), bachelor herds and breeding herds can be distinguished. During the rest of the year, territorial males join breeding or bachelor herds. Adult males establish territories during the mating season; they use communal dung heaps and scent-mark the grass and bushes with the preorbital glands. Mainly diurnal and rests in shade during the hottest part of the day.

Food Leaves and grass. Drinks water daily when available.

Breeding 1 young is born September–January after a gestation period of ±6 months. ♀ has 2 pairs of groin mammae.

Mass
♂ 47–82 kg; ♀ 32–52 kg

Shoulder height
♂ ±90 cm, ♀ ±86 cm

R.W.
Min: 23⅝", Max: 31⅞"

S.C.I.
Min: 54 pnts, Max: 67½ pnts

Age
±12 years

Vocalisation
An alarm snort. Adult males make a roaring rattle and snort, especially during mating season.

5–6 cm

Grey rhebok

Pelea capreolus
(Vaalribbok)

♂   ♀

Mass
18–23 kg

Shoulder height
±74 cm

R.W.
Min: 7⅞", Max: 11⅛"

S.C.I.
Min: 18 pnts, Max: 27¼ pnts

Age
±9 years

Vocalisation
Snorts and hisses; 'coughs' when
alarmed.

4.5 cm

Subspecies None.

Identification Long, thin neck with very long, pointed, upright ears.
The horns are straight and stand upright.

Differs from other species Mountain reedbuck: horns bent forward
and there are black spots below the ears; the neck is shorter and
thicker, and the ears are rounded.

Difference between ♂ and ♀ The male has horns, and is heavier
than the female.

Habitat Rocky mountains, mountain slopes and plateaus with
sufficient grass and a few shrubs and trees. Utilises a more exposed
habitat than the mountain reedbuck: grass slopes of the Drakensberg
1 400–2 500 m above sea level. Independent of water.

Habits Forms herds of up to 12 animals. There are solitary males
and family groups (with a territorial male), but no bachelor herds.
When a young male leaves the group, he remains solitary until he is
old enough to establish his own territory. A part of the family group's
home range is the territorial male's territory. He advertises this with
certain movements and ostentations. The rhebok grazes with short
resting periods and rests for ±3 hours during the hottest time of
the day.

Food Grass.

Breeding 1 young is born December–January after a gestation period
of ±8 months. ♀ has 2 pairs of groin mammae.

Gemsbok (Oryx)

♂

Subspecies Only one subspecies occurs in the region:

■ *O.g. gazella*

Identification Large antelope, with both sexes having long, straight horns. The face is black with white marks, and the tail is long and black.

Difference between ♂ and ♀ The male is slightly heavier than the female and the horns are thicker and usually shorter.

Habitat Associated with open, dry landscape. Prefers open grassland in semidesert areas and open, dry savannah. May even penetrate open woodland in search of new grazing areas. In the Kalahari, it prefers the sand-dune midland with scattered plant cover and short one-year grass.

Habits Nursing and mixed herds, territorial and other solitary males (1–12 animals per herd) occur. Territorial males are very tolerant of other males and often accompany mixed herds. They mark their territories by horning and scratching the ground, and defecating in a squatting position so that the dung lies in a heap to retain the smell longer.

Food Grass, sometimes also tsammas, succulent rhizomes and tubers. Subsists without water for a long time, but drinks if available. Digs for water in sand at times.

Breeding 1 young is born any time during the year after a gestation period of ±9 months. ♀ has 2 pairs of groin mammae.

Mass
♂ ±240 kg, ♀ ±210 kg

Shoulder height
±120 cm

R.W.
Min: 40", Max: 49¼"

S.C.I.
Min: 88 pnts, Max: 105 pnts

Age
±19 years

Vocalisation
Bellows like cattle.

10–13 cm

Roan antelope (Roan)

Hippotragus equinus
(Bastergemsbok)

♀

Mass
230–272 kg

Shoulder height
±143 cm

R.W.
Min: 27", Max: 39"

S.C.I.
Min: 68 pnts, Max: 73 pnts

Age
±19 years

Vocalisation
Something between a snort and a hissing sound.

11–13 cm

Subspecies Large overlap in northwestern Zimbabwe.
≡ *H.e. equinus*
▬ *H.e. cottoni*

Identification A very large antelope. Both sexes have scimitar-like horns and very long ears. The face seems to have a black mask with white patches from the corner of the eyes and around the mouth.

Difference between ♂ and ♀ The male is slightly larger than the female and its horns are thicker.

Habitat Very specific requirements: open savannah with large stretches of medium to tall grass and sufficient water. Very sensitive to change in habitat such as bush encroachment and over-utilisation of grass. Tolerates scattered short shrubs. Avoids thickets, areas with short grass and woodland with roof of foliage.

Habits Bachelor herds, solitary males and breeding herds exist (5–25 animals per herd). A breeding herd with a dominant male and female as leader will leave their home range only if food and water become scarce. The male shows territorial behaviour, but merely defends his females (300–500 m around the herd) and not a specific area. When a young male becomes an adult (at 5–6 years) he leaves the bachelor herd and goes solitary. Grazes in the early mornings and late afternoons.

Food Grass (from 2–8 cm) and sometimes also leaves.

Breeding 1 young is born any time during the year after a gestation period of 9–9½ months. ♀ has 2 pairs of groin mammae.

Sable antelope

Hippotragus niger
(Swartwitpens)

♂

Subspecies Only one subspecies occurs in the region:
- *H.n. niger*

Identification These large antelope are dark brown to black and have white bellies. The face is white with dark stripes and both sexes have scimitar-like horns.

Difference between ♂ and ♀ The female is usually browner and slightly smaller than the male, and its horns are thinner and shorter.

Habitat Shelter and water are important requirements (seldom found further than 3 km from water). Prefers open woodland or woodland near vleis or grassland with medium to tall grass, but may even be found in dense woodland on well-drained soil (where roan antelopes do not occur). Avoids dense savannah and areas with short grass.

Habits Territorial males, nursing herds and bachelor herds exist (10–30 animals per herd). A territorial male defends his area with intimidating displays. Nursing herds, with one or more dominant females as leaders, move through the territories of males. Young males (3 years) join bachelor herds and remain there until they are 5-6 years old. Grazes early in the mornings and late afternoons.

Food Mainly grass, but sometimes leaves at the end of a dry season. Drinks water at least once a day, usually between 10:00 and 16:00.

Breeding 1 young is born January–March after a gestation period of ±8 months. ♀ has 2 pairs of groin mammae.

Mass
180–250 kg

Shoulder height
±140 cm

R.W.
Min: 41⅞", Max: 55¾"

S.C.I.
Min: 100 pnts, Max: 121 pnts

Age
±17 years

Vocalisation
Snorts, bellows and sneezes.

9–11 cm

Buffalo

Cyncerus caffer
(Buffel)

♂   ♀

Mass
♂ 750–820 kg, ♀ 680–750 kg

Shoulder height
♂ ±170 cm, ♀ ±140 cm

R.W.
Min: 45", Max: 64"

S.C.I.
Min: 100 pnts, Max: 140¼ pnts

Age
±23 years

Vocalisation
Bellows like cattle, and grunts when in a fight.

12–16 cm

Subspecies Only one subspecies occurs in the region:
▇ *S.c. caffer*

Identification Large and cattle-like, with greyish-black colouring, but assumes the colour of the soil when it wallows in mud. Both male and female have horns.

Difference between ♂ and ♀ The male is usually darker and heavier than the female and has larger horns.

Habitat Enough edible grass, shade and water are important requirements. Preferential grass occurs in mopane and thornveld, as well as in other types of woodland and open vleis. Avoids floodplains or grass plains that are far from the shade of trees.

Habits Forms herds that can number a few thousand. Split into smaller herds in summer, moving apart in search of good grazing, but when it becomes drier return to areas with permanent water. Mixed and bachelor herds as well as solitary males can be distinguished. There is a definite hierarchy between males, which is maintained by threatening behaviour. Dangerous animals to hunt – a wounded buffalo may circle back, wait for the hunter along its track and attack. Grazes when it is cool and rests in the shade during the hottest part of the day.

Food Grass, drinks water regularly/twice a day (early morning and late afternoon).

Breeding 1 young is born in summer after a gestation period of ±11 months. ♀ has 2 pairs of groin mammae.

Eland

Tragelaphus oryx
(Eland)

♂ *T.o. oryx*

♀ *T.o. livingstonii*

Subspecies

■ *T.o. oryx* (without white side stripes)
■ *T.o. livingstonii* (6–7 white side stripes)
■ Large area of intergradation (1–3 white side stripes)

Identification The region's largest antelope. Resembles a Brahman with its large hump and dewlap. Both the male and female have horns. As the male ages, it becomes darker along the neck.

Difference between ♂ and ♀ The male is larger and much heavier than the female and its horns are thicker and heavier.

Habitat Very adaptable: found from semidesert shrubveld to different types of woodland and moist mountain grassland (Mozambique). Trees and shrubs are important. Avoids vast open grass plains. Independent of water.

Habits Usually forms small herds, but large herds of hundreds have been seen. The hierarchy in the herds is based on age and size. In the calving season, nursing herds and bachelor herds can be distinguished. At a later stage, young animals and males join the nursing herds and form breeding herds. Breeding herds are placid, but serious fights occur in bachelor herds. Also grazes at night. A characteristic clicking sound can be heard when they walk.

Food Mainly leaves, sometimes grass. Drinks water regularly when available.

Breeding 1 young is born any time during the year (peaking August–October) after a gestation period of ±9 months. ♀ has 2 pairs of groin mammae.

Mass
♂ ±700 kg, ♀ ±460 kg

Shoulder height
♂ ±170 cm, ♀ ±150 cm

R.W.
Min: 35″, Max: 45″

S.C.I.
Min: 77 pnts, Max: 110 pnts

Age
±12 years

Vocalisation
Females moo, calves bleat; adults bellow, bark and grumble.

11–13 cm

Greater kudu

Tragelaphus strepsiceros
(Koedoe)

♂

♀

Mass
♂ 190–270 kg, ♀ 120–210 kg

Shoulder height
♂ ±150 cm, ♀ ±135 cm

R.W.
Min: 53⅜", Max: 73⅛"

S.C.I.
Min: 121 pnts, Max: 154 pnts

Age
±14 years

Vocalisation
A very loud, hoarse 'cough'.

8–9.5 cm

Subspecies Only one subspecies occurs in the region:

■ *T.s. strepsiceros*

Identification A large, elegant antelope, with impressive horns and white stripes on the flanks. The female has prominent ears. The male becomes darker along the neck as the hair falls out.

Difference between ♂ and ♀ The female is smaller than the male, and has no horns.

Habitat A savannah species: occurs even in dry semidesert areas that have sufficient food and shrubs for shelter. Prefers open woodland (especially thornveld) and rocky terrain with water nearby. Prefers wooded areas along streams in dry areas.

Habits Form herds of 4–12 animals, consisting of females and their young or males. In the mating season, an adult male is accompanied by a few females and young. Out of season, the males go solitary or form bachelor herds of up to 6 animals. Grazes in the early mornings and late afternoons; rests in the shade during the hottest part of the day. Very timid and takes off to shelter at the slightest sign of danger. When it runs away, its tail is turned upwards so that the white underparts show – a sign of alarm and direction.

Food Leaves, sometimes sprouts, pods (especially of thorn trees) and even fresh grass.

Breeding 1 young is born any time during the year, peaking in late summer after a gestation period of ±7 months. ♀ has 2 pairs of groin mammae.

Sitatunga

Tragelaphus spekei
(Sitatunga / Waterkoedoe)

♂

♀

Subspecies Only one subspecies occurs in the region:
■ *T.s. selousi*

Identification A large semi-aquatic antelope, resembling a nyala. The hooves are long and splayed. The male has a chevron mark between its eyes.

Differs from other species Bushbuck (Chobe): smaller, more reddish and does not live in swamps; the male has smaller horns.

Difference between ♂ and ♀ Only the male has horns, while the female is usually a lighter colour and is much smaller.

Habitat Lives mostly in the water even up to 1 m deep. Prefers papyrus and common reed beds in swamps or flooded areas of the Okavango and Chobe rivers. Grazes in shallow water on watergrass but avoids open floodplains.

Habits Lives in small herds of up to 6 animals, with a male or females and young; they spread out when grazing. Single animals also occur. Grazes throughout the day, but rests during the hottest part of the day on platforms of flattened reeds and other debris in the papyrus. Moves out at night to the surrounding woodland or islands, but returns before dawn. Are very good swimmers.

Food Watergrass, papyrus, reed shoots and fresh leaves.

Breeding 1 young is born any time during the year (peaking June–July). ♀ has 2 pairs of groin mammae.

Mass
♂ ±114 kg, ♀ ±55 kg

Shoulder height
♂ ±114 cm, ♀ ±90 cm

R.W.
Min: 27⅛", Max: 32½"

S.C.I.
Min: 60 pnts, Max: 84¼ pnts

Age
±19 years

Vocalisation
Drawn-out alarm bark (similar to bushbuck), which is repeated.

← 7–8.5 cm →

Nyala

Tragelaphus angasii
(Njala)

♂ ♀

Mass
♂ 92–126 kg, ♀ 55–68 kg

Shoulder height
♂ ±112 cm, ♀ ±97 cm

R.W.
Min: 27", Max: 32¾"

S.C.I.
Min: 63 pnts, Max: 84½ pnts

Age
±13 years

Vocalisation
The female makes a 'click' sound, and young ones bleat. A deep bark as an alarm call.

5–6 cm

Subspecies None.

Identification An elegant, slender antelope. The male has a white chevron mark between the eyes, white-tipped mane and yellow 'socks'.

Differs from other species Bushbuck: female is smaller and browner than the nyala female, usually without stripes.

Difference between ♂ and ♀ Only the male has horns. The female is lighter in colour and much smaller.

Habitat Associated with thickets in dry woodland. This includes dense woodland, riverine forests, island bush in floodplains and other thickets. Surrounding floodplains and grass plains are visited when grass sprouts. Dependent on water.

Habits Forms temporary herds of 3–30 animals with home ranges overlapping. Solitary young ones, females and males; young male herds, adult male herds, female herds, family herds and mixed herds can be distinguished. Family herds are the most stable. The male horns the ground or lifts its mane when another male is nearby. Grazes when it is cool, even at night, and rests during the hottest part of the day.

Food Leaves, branches, fruit and flowers. Drinks water daily when available.

Breeding 1 young is born any time during the year (peaking August–December), after a gestation period of 7 months. ♀ has 2 pairs of groin mammae.

Bushbuck

Tragelaphus scriptus
(Bosbok)

♂ *T.s. sylvaticus*

♂ *T.s. ornatus* Chobe bushbuck

♀ *T.s. roualeyni* Limpopo bushbuck

Subspecies

T.s. ornatus (reddish-brown, white side stripes)
T.s. roualeyni (more brown than abovementioned)
T.s. sylvaticus (darkest)

Identification A timid, medium-sized antelope, with white spots on the buttocks, against the legs, at the base of the neck and against the throat.

Differs from other species Nyala: female is larger and more yellow, with white stripes. Sitatunga: larger than Chobe bushbuck, not as reddish-brown and lives in swamps.

Difference between ♂ and ♀ Only the male has horns, and it is larger and darker than the female.

Habitat Prefers riverine forests or other types of dense thickets near perennial water. May move in summer to other thickets near temporary water sources, returning when it becomes dry. Dependent on water and sufficient shelter.

Habits Usually solitary, but occasionally seen in pairs, small groups of females, females with their young, or small bachelor herds. Stays in riverine forest during the winter when it has a smaller home range than in the wet season. Usually grazes at night or early mornings and late afternoons and rests during the day in thickets. Has keen senses. The male is very brave and will attack even when wounded.

Food Mainly leaves. Also grass, branches, flowers and fruit.

Breeding 1 young is born any time during the year after a gestation period of ±6 months. ♀ has 2 pairs of groin mammae.

Mass
♂ 40–77 kg, ♀ 30–36 kg

Shoulder height
♂ ±80 cm, ♀ ±70 cm

R.W.
Min: 15", Max: 18¼"

S.C.I.
Min: 33 pnts, Max: 52 pnts

Age
±11 years

Vocalisation
Grumbles and has a loud hoarse bark as an alarm call.

4–6 cm

99

Mountain reedbuck

Redunca fulvorufula
(Rooiribbok)

♂

♀

Mass
♂ 24–36 kg, ♀ 15–34 kg

Shoulder height
♂ ±75 cm, ♀ ±73 cm

R.W.
Min: 6⅛", Max: 10"

S.C.I.
Min: 11 pnts, Max: 17¼ pnts

Age
±11 years

Vocalisation
A shrill whistle similar to that of the reedbuck.

4.5 cm

Subspecies Only one subspecies occurs in the region:
■ *R.f. fulvorufula*

Identification A medium-sized antelope, with a black spot below each ear. The colour of the body is greyish with a red sheen and the neck is brown. The points of the ears are rounded.

Differs from other species Grey rhebok: the neck is also grey, but is longer and thinner; horns are straight and the ears are more upright and pointed. Reedbuck: larger, of a brighter yellow, with black stripes on the forelegs; prefers marshy areas.

Difference between ♂ and ♀ Female is smaller than the male and has no horns.

Habitat Associated with mountainous areas. Dry rocky slopes of mountains and hills with sufficient grass and shelter such as scattered trees and shrubs. Usually avoids open plateaus and peaks. Dependent on water.

Habits Usually forms herds of 3–6 (sometimes up to 30). Territorial males, other solitary males, nursing herds and bachelor herds can be distinguished. Nursing herds are unstable and move over the territories of several males. Grazes when it is cool – even at night – and rests in the shade during the hottest part of the day. When alarmed, it flees downhill, while the grey rhebok flees to higher areas.

Food Mainly grass. Drinks water regularly, especially in dry, warm weather.

Breeding 1 young is born any time during the year (peaking December–January) after a gestation period of ±8 months. ♀ has 2 pairs of groin mammae.

Reedbuck (Southern reedbuck)

Redunca arundinum
(Rietbok)

♂

♀

Subspecies Only one subspecies occurs in the region:

■ *R.a. arundinum*

Identification A medium-sized antelope, with yellowish grey-brown colouration and sometimes black spots below the ears. The front of the forelegs is dark brown.

Differs from other species Mountain reedbuck: smaller greyish and prefers mountainous habitat. Impala: redder; three black stripes: two on the buttocks and one on the tail.

Difference between ♂ and ♀ Only the male has horns and it is larger than the female.

Habitat Always in or near vleis or reed beds with open water. Also floodplains and other grass plains (with tall grass) along rivers or marshes with perennial water. Avoids thickets and woodland. Dependent on water and reeds for shelter.

Habits Usually lives in pairs, occupying a territory. Although larger groups are found, reedbuck are not gregarious. Territorial male defends his area with threatening displays. He defecates and urinates in front of his challenger, standing on stiff legs with the head held high. Younger male shows his submission to territorial male by bowing his head. If grazing is in a good condition, it becomes nocturnal; and more diurnal during the dry season.

Food Mainly grass. Drinks water regularly, even more than once a day on warm days.

Breeding 1 young is born any time during the year after a gestation period of 7–8 months. ♀ has 2 pairs of groin mammae.

Mass
♂ ±80 kg, ♀ ±70 kg

Shoulder height
♂ ±90 cm, ♀ ±80 cm

R.W.
Min: 14", Max: 18⅝"

S.C.I.
Min: 21 pnts, Max: 32½ pnts

Age
±9 years

Vocalisation
A high-pitched whistle through the nostrils as an alarm call.

5.5 cm

Waterbuck

Kobus ellipsiprymnus
(Waterbok)

♂   ♀

Mass
♂ 250–270 kg, ♀ 205–250 kg

Shoulder height
♂ ±170 cm, ♀ ±130 cm

R.W.
Min: 28", Max: 39¼"

S.C.I.
Min: 71 pnts, Max: 91¾ pnts

Age
±14 years

Vocalisation
Snorts; female calls her calf with a soft *moo*.

8–9 cm

Subspecies Only one subspecies occurs in the region:
▪ *K.e. ellipsiprymnus*

Identification Large greyish-brown antelope, with a white circle around the tail. The hair is coarse, shaggy and long.

Difference between ♂ and ♀ The female is smaller than the male and does not have horns.

Habitat A savannah species: never far away from water, but usually avoids riverine forests. Found in woodland along rivers, dry floodplains and vleis or in reed beds along marshes. These areas usually have good-quality grass for grazing. Very dependent on water.

Habits Usually forms herds of 6–12 (even up to 30). Territorial males, nursing herds and bachelor herds occur. Herds become larger in summer, but divide in winter. Young males become full grown at about 5–6 years and then try to establish a territory. Territories are defended by threatening displays. A subordinate male lowers its head as a sign of submission. Serious fights are very common. If a nursing herd passes across a male's territory, the male will try to round up the females.

Food Mainly grass, but sometimes leaves and fruit. Drinks water regularly.

Breeding 1 (occasionally 2) young are born any time during the year after a gestation period of ±9 months. ♀ has 2 pairs of groin mammae.

Red lechwe

Kobus leche
(Rooi lechwe / Basterwaterbok)

♂

♀

Subspecies Only one subspecies occurs in the region:
■ *K.l. leche*

Identification A medium-sized antelope, with characteristic dark markings on the forelegs. The shoulders are lower than the croup, and the body slants forward.

Differs from other species Puku: smaller, more gold-brown, less white on the belly and without the dark markings on the forelegs.

Difference between ♂ and ♀ The female is smaller and has no horns.

Habitat Always in or near water. On shallow floodplains (up to 50 cm deep) along swamps and rivers, or in areas between papyrus or reed beds and the start of dry land. Uses areas with shallower water than the sitatunga.

Habits Usually form herds of 10–30. Larger aggregations sometimes occur. Bachelor herds, nursing herds and solitary adult males can be distinguished. During the mating season, a few males establish small territories, which they share with some nursing herds so as to establish a breeding area. Other males are allowed if they are not interested in the male's females, or else driven out by threatening displays. Usually grazes in the early mornings and late afternoons and rests on dry ground during the heat of day.

Food Watergrass and other grass. Drinks water regularly (up to 3 times a day).

Breeding 1 young is born any time during the year (peaking October–December) after a gestation period of 7–8 months. ♀ has 2 pairs of groin mammae.

Mass
♂ 100–130 kg, ♀ 61–97 kg

Shoulder height
♂ ±104 cm, ♀ ±97 cm

R.W.
Min: 26", Max: 35"

S.C.I.
Min: 58 pnts, Max: 76½ pnts

Age
Unknown

Vocalisation
A low whistle and a whinnying grunt as an alarm call.

7.5 cm

Puku

♂   ♀

Mass
♂ 68–91 kg, ♀ 48–80 kg

Shoulder height
♂ ±81 cm, ♀ ±78 cm

R.W.
Min: 16⅜", Max: 22⅜"

S.C.I.
Min: 46 pnts, Max: 58 pnts

Age
Unknown

Vocalisation
An alarm whistle, which is repeated up to 5 times.

Subspecies Only one subspecies occurs in the region:

■ *K.v. vardonii*

Identification A medium-sized antelope, with a golden-brown colour virtually all over the body; the belly, throat and areas around the mouth are whitish.

Differs from other species Red lechwe: larger, reddish-brown, more white on the belly, with black markings against the forelegs. Impala: a brighter red, with 3 black stripes on the buttocks and tail.

Difference between ♂ and ♀ The female is smaller and has no horns.

Habitat A specialised habitat of grass areas directly along or around water. Utilises the narrow stretches of grass plains between marsh or floodplains and the woodland on surrounding higher ground. Dependent on water.

Habits Forms herds with loose associations of 2–28. Territorial males, female herds and bachelor herds can be distinguished. Territories are not defended all the time, and sexually inactive males are allowed. If a female herd passes through a male's territory, he will try to round them up. Bachelor herds' home ranges are separate from those of the females and territorial males. Grazes in the early mornings and late afternoons until after sunset. Often seen together with impala.

Food Mainly grass.

Breeding 1 young is born any time during the year (peaking May–September), after a gestation period of ±8 months. ♀ has 2 pairs of groin mammae.

Ground pangolin (Scaly ant-eater)

Manis temminckii
(Ietermagog / Ietermagô)

Subspecies None.

Identification Very hard and strong imbricated scales all over the body, except the underparts and the sides of the face, which are bare. Has well-developed claws on the forepaws.

Difference between ♂ and ♀ None.

Habitat Occurs in a variety of habitat types: from bushy veld in the arid parts (250 mm per annum) to different types of woodlands in humid savannah areas. Occurs also on rocky hills, sandveld and floodplain grassland. Ants and termites (on which it feeds) and shelter (such as holes in the ground or piles of leaf debris in which to rest) are important requirements.

Habits Mainly noctural and solitary. Walks on its hind legs, balancing so that the tail and forelegs touch the ground only now and then. Very shy and stands dead still if disturbed. If followed, stands stretched on its hind legs, supported by the tail, to scan the vicinity. Rolls into a tight ball when in danger. Rests during the day in either old antbear or springhare holes, rock crevices or in piles of leaf debris.

Food Mainly ants, sometimes termites. Has a very long sticky tongue and no teeth.

Breeding 1 young is born May–July after a gestation period of ±4 months. ♀ has 1 pair of groin mammae.

Mass
4.5–14.5 kg

Length
±81 cm

Age
±12 years

Vocalisation
Unknown

7 cm

105

Scrub hare

Lepus saxatilis
(Kolhaas)

Mass
♂ 1.4–3.8 kg, ♀ 1.6–4.5 kg

Length
±55 cm

Age
±7 years

Vocalisation
Usually silent. A loud
scream when handled.

3 cm

Subspecies 6 subspecies occur in the south of its distribution area, and are not easily identified. Examples in southwestern Cape are larger and become smaller with smaller ears towards the northwestern Cape.

Identification The larger of the two hares. Dull yellow with greyish speckled (salt-and-pepper effect); name brown to orange, with a white patch on the forehead.

Differs from other species Cape hare: smaller and does not occur in scrub, preferring open dry grassland.

Difference between ♂ and ♀ The male is slightly smaller.

Habitat Savannah species: scrub areas with patches of grass. Avoids dense bush or open grass plains. Grazes at night in open areas. Sufficient edible grass and dense shrub for shelter are important requirements. Independent of water.

Habits Mainly nocturnal, but may graze in the mornings on cool, overcast days. Sensitive to cold weather: seldom seen on cold nights and remains in its shelter if it rains. Rests during the day beneath a shrub with some grass close by. Lies down with its ears flat and the head placed close to the body and leaps up when danger is very near. Runs with a swerving and turning movement. Usually solitary, but in mating season one or more males keep close to a female.

Food Grass and rhizomes. Prefers green grass. Gets enough moisture from food.

Breeding 1–3 young are born any time during the year (peaking September–February) after a gestation period of ±5 weeks.

Cape hare

Lepus capensis
(Vlakhaas)

Subspecies 16 subspecies: very difficult to distinguish. Examples from the desert and semidesert areas are usually smaller and paler.
Identification The smallest of the two hares. Colour varies a lot, but the tail is usually dull black on top and white underneath.
Differs from other species Scrub hare: larger and usually has a white patch on the forehead; also prefers a denser environment.
Difference between ♂ and ♀ The male is slightly smaller than the female.
Habitat Prefers open dry areas, grass plains in the vicinity of pans and other grassy areas. Edible grass and shelter, such as low shrubs or tufts of grass, in which to rest, are essential. Independent of water.
Habits Although mainly nocturnal, also seen on cool, overcast days. Less active in cold weather. Does not appear when it rains. Rests during the day, lying beneath a shrub or tuft of grass with the ears flat, dependent on its camouflage. Jumps into antbear or springhare holes when fleeing – something a scrub hare does not do. Usually solitary. In mating season, males may fight over a female.
Food Only grass, especially short grass. Gets enough moisture from food and dew.
Breeding 1–3 young are born any time during the year (peaking in summer) after a gestation period of ±6 weeks.

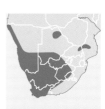

Mass
♂ 1.4–1.8 kg, ♀ 1.5–2.3 kg

Length
±47 cm

Age
±5 years

Vocalisation
Usually silent. Snorts or screams when handled.

3 cm

Smith's red rock rabbit

Pronolagus rupestris
(Smith se rooiklipkonyn)

Mass
1.3–2.0 kg

Length
±82 cm

Age
Unknown

Vocalisation
Makes a shrill scream if frightened.

Subspecies 7 subspecies are described, but are under dispute.

Identification This one is the smallest of the three species of red rock rabbits. The reddish brown coat is thick and coarse and has typical black and white speckles. The tail and legs are reddish brown.

Differs from other species Hares: their tails white with black on top.

Difference between ♂ and ♀ Males are larger than females.

Habitat Confined to stony hills and koppies and rocky ridges with short, sparse vegetation and enough edible grass, suitable to their requirements.

Habits Nocturnal and forage alone, but are usually part of a group with communal dung heaps. Emerge well after sunset and forage through the night, but do not stray far away from their rocky habitat. They rest during the day underneath big rocks; sometimes in thick stances of grass. They make their nests in the open, with the entrance against a bush.

Food Grass, especially new green grass after a veld fire.

Breeding 1–2 young are born in summer after a gestation period of 5–6 weeks.

2.5 cm

Springhare

Pedetes capensis
(Springhaas)

Subspecies Only one subspecies occurs in the region:

▇ *P.c. capensis*

Identification Resembles a kangaroo, with long hind legs for leaping and short forelegs. The tail ends in a characteristic black broad tip.

Difference between ♂ **and** ♀ None.

Habitat Compacted sandy soil for digging holes. Areas with precipitations of sandy silt along rivers is an important requirement. Also found in sandy country or sandy shrubveld. Avoids hard clay soil. Holes are usually on higher ground. Independent of water.

Habits Nocturnal: only appears when it is quite dark. Keen excavators; loosening the soil with the forelegs, and working it out with the hind legs. The burrows in which they live slope down for a few metres and, at a depth of about 1 m, become level again. On the farthest side, an escape hole is dug. Burrows may have corridors and more than one entrance and emergency exit. Only one springhare lives in a hole. There will be tracks on the heap of soil outside the hole if it is occupied. Grazes up to 400 m from the burrow. In cold weather, it does not leave its hole.

Food Seeds, stems, leaves, tubers and rhizomes of grass.

Breeding 1 (occasionally 2) young are born 2–3 times a year after a gestation period of ±10 weeks. ♀ has 1 pair of pectoral mammae.

Mass
2.5–3.8 kg

Length
±80 cm

Age
±7 years

Vocalisation
Usually silent, but screams loudly when handled.

3.5 cm

Tree squirrel

Paraxerus cepapi
(Boomeekhoring)

Mass
♂ 76–240 g, ♀ 108–265 g

Length
±35 cm

Age
±8 years

Vocalisation
Bird-like *cheek-chik-chik-chik*
sounds and chattering.

2.5 cm

Subspecies colour lighter in arid areas than in moist areas.

- *P.c. cepapi*
- *P.c. cepapoides*
- *P.c. phalaena*
- *P.c. maunensis*
- *P.c. tsumebensis*
- *P.c. carpi*
- *P.c. chobiensis*
- *P.c. sindi*
- *P.c. kalaharicus*

Identification A well-known savannah squirrel. Greyish-brown speckled with a long bushy tail and yellow on the flanks.

Differs from other species Red squirrel: tail, legs and belly more yellow or reddish than the body. Sun squirrel: larger, and full length of tail is ringed with a lighter colour.

Difference between ♂ and ♀ None.

Habitat In most types of savannah, especially mopane and thornveld and mixed savannah. As it requires holes in tree trunks in which to rest or make a nest, old mopane and thorn trees are popular. Independent of water.

Habits Usually solitary. They live in groups of a few adults and young ones defining an area and marking it with scent. Groom and scent-mark one another and chase away strangers. If a predator is seen, it takes off to a safe place and teases predator with chattering and flicking of tail. Grazes on the ground and is always alert, fleeing to the nest or tree at the slightest disturbance – always keeping the tree between itself and the threat.

Food Leaves, seeds, fruit, flowers, bar, thorn-tree gum, lichen and insects.

Breeding 1–3 young born any time during the year (peaking October–April) after a gestation period of ±8 weeks. ♀ has 3 pairs of mammae.

Ground squirrel

Xerus inauris
(Waaierstert-grondeekhoring)

Subspecies None.

Identification Characteristic white stripes on its sides, and a white belly. The 'fan' tail is bushy, white and brown, and is sometimes spread over the squirrel's back for shade.

Differs from other species Mountain ground squirrel: looks the same, but its burrows are mostly on rocky hills or banks of rocks, which are avoided by the ground squirrel.

Difference between ♂ and ♀ The male is heavier than the female.

Habitat Only found in dry areas. Prefers open country with scattered bushes on hard or calcareous soil (avoids loose sandy soil). Also found along dry streams on dry floodplains or in open Karooveld. Independent of water.

Habits Gregarious: forms colonies of up to 30, and lives in a burrow, which it digs with different entrances, rooms and corridors. Rooms are layered with grass on which to rest. Colonies consist of females and their young. Males move between groups and stay only temporarily. They sometimes share the burrows with the suricate and/or yellow mongoose. Diurnal: only appears after sunrise and returns before sunset. They often groom themselves and one another.

Food Grass, leaves, tubers, seeds, roots, stems and sometimes insects.

Breeding 1–3 young are born any time during the year after a gestation period of ±7 weeks. ♀ has 2 pairs of groin mammae.

Mass
♂ 511–1022 g, ♀ 511–795 g

Length
±45 cm

Age
±15 years

Vocalisation
High-pitched whistle or scream as alarm. Aggressive grumble.

Porcupine

Hystrix africaeaustralis
(Ystervark)

Mass
♂ 10–19 kg, ♀ 10–24 kg

Length
±84 cm

Age
±20 years

Vocalisation
Rattles the tail quills, grunts, sniffs and chatters the teeth.

Subspecies None.

Identification The region's largest rodent. The body is covered with characteristic sharp, black-and-white quills and flattened bristles.

Difference between ♂ and ♀ None.

Habitat Very adaptable: found in most of the vegetation areas. Prefers broken veld with rocky hills and rocky reefs. Shelters in caves, crevices, antbear and other holes, which it adapts. Sometimes a large number of bones – which have been carried there – can be seen around the holes. Independent of water.

Habits Although three or four make use of the same shelter, they often roam alone. Nocturnal, but lies in the sun at the edge of its shelter. Stands quite still when disturbed and is often overlooked. Moves noisily down footpaths as it rubs, grunts and sniffs. A noisy grazer. Attacks instinctively sideways or backwards so that the quills remain facing the attacker. Appears clumsy, but can run quickly.

Food Digs for tubers, bulbs and roots. Fruit, bark, carrion and vegetables.

Breeding 1–3 young are born any time during the year (August–March in summer rainfall areas) after a gestation period of ±3 months. ♀ has 2 pairs of pectoral mammae to the sides.

7.5–9 cm

Greater cane rat

Thryonomys swinderianus
(Groot rietrot)

Subspecies None.

Identification Largest of the two cane rats. Brown with yellow speckles and spine hair. The elongated snout hangs over the nostrils.

Differs from other species Lesser cane rat: smaller and the tail is much shorter than that of the greater cane rate. Utilises a different habitat.

Difference between ♂ and ♀ The male is larger than the female.

Habitat Specialised requirements: Reed beds along rivers and dams or tall, thick-stemmed grass in the vicinity of vleis, lakes, dams, floodplains or rivers. Dependent on water. Frequents sugarcane plantations.

Habits Lives in small groups of 8–10 animals, but grazes alone. Mainly nocturnal, but also active at dawn. Tramples clear footpaths between reed beds and tall grass, where it can move unseen. Rests in thick shelter of reeds or in holes in the river bank or beneath thick vegetation. If chased along the footpath, it runs a distance, stops until the pursuer is close and repeats the action. Swims very well.

Food Roots, stems and sprouts of reeds and grass.

Breeding 4–8 young are born August–December after a gestation period of 4–5 months. ♀ has 3 pairs of pectoral mammae.

Mass
♂ ±4.54 kg, ♀ ±3.58 kg

Length
♂ ±72 cm, ♀ ±67 cm

Age
Unknown

Vocalisation
Snorts when it grazes. Stamps rear paws and makes a loud whistle as an alarm.

6.5 cm

Lesser red musk shrew

Crocidura hirta
(Kleinrooiskeerbek)

Mass
15–17 g

Length
±15 cm

Age
±18 months

Vocalisation
A loud squeak.

Identification The colour varies from (a speckled) cinnamon-brown to light reddish brown and dark brown. The underparts are pale dull-yellow. Animals from the western parts of its distribution are lighter in colour than those from the east.

Differs from other species Greater musk shrew: is much larger with a more southerly distribution.

Difference between ♂ and ♀ Males tend to be slightly heavier than females.

Habitat The dark eastern race occurs in dense riverine thickets. The western race occurs in parts with low bushes in the open scrub of Botswana. Prefers shelter like dense thickets, fallen tree trunks and piles of rotten plant material such as compost heaps in suburban gardens.

Habits Mainly nocturnal, but in a way diurnal as well; with a peak in activity just after sunset and again just before sunrise. Forage alone, but is usually part of a pair or a small group. They sleep during the day underneath piles of dry plant material or in old debris along rivers.

Food Mainly insects; but they feed on lizards, plant material, earth worms and termites as well.

Breeding 1–9 young are born from September–May after a gestation period of 18 days.

Eastern rock elephant shrew

Elephantulus myurus
(Oostelike klipklaasneus)

Identification The upperparts are yellowish grey and turn grey towards the flanks. Around the eyes are distinct white rings. The ears are brown and the underparts white. The forefeet and hind feet have 5 toes.

Differs from other species Western rock elephant shrew: has a hairier tail and more distinct lighter patches behind the ears.

Difference between ♂ and ♀ None

Habitat Is confined to rocky koppies or big piles of rocks, with holes or crevices for shelter. Prefers areas with overhanging rock surfaces or plant cover that can supply protection against aerial predators.

Habits Pairs occupy large exclusive home ranges. Although sometimes active during the day, they are mainly nocturnal, with a peak in activity at dusk and dawn. They run very fast, and can jump up to ±1 metre between rocks. Early in the morning, before they start foraging, they enjoy sunbathing on a rock. They are fond of drumming on the ground with their feet.

Food Insects: preferring ants and termites.

Breeding 1, usually 2 young are born September–April.

Mass
±60 g

Length
±26 cm

Age
±4 years

Vocalisation
High-pitched squeaks as alarm signal.

Gambian (Peters's) epauletted fruit bat

Epomophorus gambianus
(Gambiese witkolvrugtevlermuis)

Mass
♂ 140 g, ♀ 80 g

Length
♂ 15 cm, ♀ 12 cm

Age
21 years

Vocalisation
Monotonous *ping-ping-ping* sounds.

Identification Colour varies between yellow brown and pale-brown, and the underparts are lighter. Both sexes have white areas at the base of the ears. But only mature males have the white epaulettes on the shoulders, visible when it calls.

Differs from other species Wahlberg's epauletted fruit bat: very much the same, but it is bigger and stockier in build.

Difference between ♂ and ♀ Males are much bigger, and have the white epaulettes on the shoulders.

Habitat Are dependant on fruit-carrying trees, like fig trees. Occur mainly in evergreen forest with high rainfall, but also along riverine vegetation, deep into otherwise unsuitable country. They are independent of water.

Habits They live in groups of up to a few hundred animals. During the day they hang (rest) upside down with their feet on the thinner branches of an evergreen tree like a fig tree or a sausage tree. Males vocalise by making a piercing *ping-ping-ping* sound – louder than that of Wahlberg's epauletted fruit bat.

Food: Are fond of the succulent fruit of wild fig, maroela, jackalberry and red milkwood.

Breeding 1 (seldom 2) young are born early in summer. ♀ has 2 pairs of abdominal mammae.

Mauritian tomb bat

Taphozous mauritianus
(Witlyfvlermuis)

Identification The upperparts are speckled grey brown and the underparts are white. The white area on the underparts reaches the undertail and wing membrane. The bat looks quite slim because of the short hair that lies flat against the body. The eyes are relatively large.

Difference between ♂ and ♀ Males are slightly smaller than females.

Habitat Occur mainly in open savannah in high rainfall areas. In parts of Eastern Zimbabwe and Mozambique, it is present up to the edge of forest.

Habits They live in pairs. Up to 3 pairs use a suitable resting site with good shelter during the day. They usually rest against a tree trunk or rock face. The resting site should give protection against the sun and rain, and could be recognised, after years of use, by the brown stains of the urine of the bats. They will (unlike other bats) try to catch a passing butterfly during the day.

Food Mainly moths, also flying termites and other insects which are caught in flight.

Breeding 1 young is born in summer.

Mass
±28 g

Length
±11 cm

Age
Unknown

Vocalisation
Chirruping while at rest; screeching when aggressive.

African molerat

Cryptomys hottentotus
(Knaagdiermol)

Mass
±13 g

Length
±15 cm

Age
±5–10 years (in captivity)

Vocalisation
Unknown

Identification The colour of the upperparts varies from cinnamon-brown to dark brown, and the underparts are lighter in colour. Some individuals have a white patch on the forehead.

Difference between ♂ and ♀ Females are usually heavier than males.

Habitat They live in a variety of soil types: from sandy to heavy compacted soils but not in heavy clayish soils. They prefer sandy alluvium along rivers. Utilise various habitats: from open grassland to dense forest.

Habits They are gregarious, living in groups of up to 10 animals. Such a group occupies a burrow which can be identified by the fresh soil at the entrance. When inside, they block the entrance with a plug of soil to prevent intruders entering.

Food Roots, bulbs and underground stolons of grasses.

Breeding 1–5 young are born any time of the year.

Brants' whistling rat

Parotomys brantsii
(Brants se fluitrot)

Identification The colour of the upperparts varies from pale yellow-brown to reddish brown; the underparts are always much lighter.
Difference between ♂ **and** ♀ None.
Habitat They are associated with the drier parts of the subregion. Prefer areas with deep, dry compacted sandy soil with sparse vegetation cover.
Habits Mainly diurnal and gregarious. A male and a number of females with their young occupy a burrow, which they dig themselves. Such a burrow has various entrances, chambers, tunnels and escape routes. The well-known sharp warning whistle, followed by drumming with the hind feet, makes everyone scatter for a burrow. The temperature in these burrows doesn't fluctuate much, and helps the rats to survive the harsh climate on the outside.
Food Vegetarians: they live on grass, seeds and stems of shrubs in the vicinity of the burrow.
Breeding 1–3 young are born in the burrow during summer. The young keeps attached to the mother's nipples when a female moves along in search of food.

Mass
90–155 g

Length
22–27 cm

Age
2–4 years (in captivity)

Vocalisation
High-pitched whistle.

Four-striped grass mouse

Rhabdomys pumilio
(Streepmuis)

Mass
30–55g

Length
±19cm

Age
4–5years (in captivity)

Vocalisation
Unknown

Identification The colour varies from pale reddish-brown in the west to dark grey-brown in the east of its distribution. Four diagnostic dark parallel lines extend from its neck to the rump.

Differs from other species Single-striped grass mouse: has only one dark line down the mid back.

Difference between ♂ and ♀ None.

Habitat A grassland species that utilises various habitats with areas of good grass cover, even in areas with a fairly well-developed shrub cover.

Habits Mainly diurnal, with a peak in activity early in the morning and late in the afternoon. They dig their own burrows underneath layered grass or at the base of a bush. From here they use footpaths to their feeding grounds. They enter areas with human activities and become commensal with man.

Food Seeds and other succulent plant material.

Breeding 2–9 young are born in summer, after a gestation period of ±3 weeks.

Single-striped grass mouse

Lemniscomys rosalia
(Eenstreepmuis)

Identification The colour varies from orange-brown in the east, to pale grey-brown in the west of its distribution. The underparts are white and there is a diagnostic single dark line down the mid back.

Differs from other species Four-striped grass mouse: this species has 4 dark lines on its back.

Difference between ♂ and ♀ Males are slightly bigger than females.

Habitat Areas with patches of grassland is a strong recommendation. This grassland can be part of different habitat types: from moist woodland to dry Kalahari scrub. They avoid areas with short grass.

Habits Diurnal and terrestrial. They dig their own burrow underneath thick layers of grass. One mouse, a pair or a family group occupies such a burrow. They move with well-used footpaths to their favourite feeding grounds.

Food Mainly plant material and seeds; sometimes also insects.

Breeding 2–8 young are born from September–March.

Mass
♂ 56–63 g, ♀ 51–58 g

Length
25–27 cm

Age
Unknown

Vocalisation
Unknown

Acacia rat

Mass
±75 g

Length
±27 cm

Age
3½ years (in captivity)

Vocalisation
Loud chattering of teeth when threatened.

Identification The colour of the upperparts is brown-grey, and the flanks are grey. The underparts are white. Around the eyes are dark rings, and the tail is brown.

Differs from other species Black-tailed tree rat: This species is more greyish, has bigger ears and a black tail.

Difference between ♂ and ♀ Males are slightly bigger than females.

Habitat Occur in acacia woodland; they prefer to live in these trees.

Habits Nocturnal. They make a nest in a hollow tree trunk, in which up to eight of these rats live. After sunset they start foraging: they first move towards the outside of the tree where they feed on the thin branches with new sprouts. From here they sometimes jump to adjacent trees to forage there. Although they prefer acacia trees, they sometimes feed on the thin branches of other trees like mopani and leadwood as well.

Food They prefer the young leaves of acacia trees and the soft green shell of their pods. They feed sometimes on insects as well.

Breeding 2–5 young are born during summer.

Black-tailed tree rat

Thallomys nigricauda
(Swartstertboomrot)

Identification The colour of the upperparts is grey, the ears are relative big and the underparts are white. The tail is black.

Differs from other species Acacia rat: more brownish, with smaller ears and a brown tail.

Difference between ♂ and ♀ Males are slightly smaller than females.

Habitat Various types of acacia woodland: They prefer areas where camel-thorn trees occur.

Habits They make a nest in a hollow branch of an acacia tree, with the entrance usually in a fork of the branch. They line the nest with soft grass, and sometimes some of this grass can be seen from the outside. One rat, a pair or a family group sleep here during the day. They start foraging after sunset on the thin branches of the tree and jump sometimes to adjacent trees to feed.

Food Prefer acacia leaves and the soft shell of the pods. They feed on insects as well.

Breeding 2–5 young are born in summer.

Mass
±80 g

Length
±31 cm

Age
3½ years (in captivity)

Vocalisation
Loud chattering of teeth.

Woodland dormouse

Graphiurus murinus
(Boswaaierstertmuis)

Mass
±28 g

Length
±16 cm

Age
±4 years

Vocalisation
Unknown

Identification A squirrel-like mouse with a distinctive thick woolly tail. The upperparts are grey and the underparts and throat are white. Around the eyes are dark patches.

Difference between ♂ and ♀ None.

Habitat They occur in woodland with rocky koppies or loose boulders between the trees. They prefer areas with acacia species with holes in the trunk or in the branches. They live in roofs of houses and especially in thatched roofs of huts.

Habits Nocturnal. They sleep during the day in holes in trees or cavities in branches of especially acacia species. These animals are more tree-living than terrestrial. They forage alone at night, looking for insects and other food.

Food Insects, grass and seeds.

Breeding 1–3 young are born in summer.

Namaqua rock mouse

Micaelamys namaquensis
(Namakwalandse klipmuis)

Identification The colour of the upperparts varies from reddish-brown to yellow brown, and the underparts are light grey.

Difference between ♂ and ♀ Females are slightly larger than males.

Habitat Occur in a variety of bushveld habitats. They prefer rocky koppies, stony outcrops and rocky hill slopes with boulders. Also occur in rocky areas in the Kalahari scrub.

Habits Nocturnal. They are gregarious, living in small colonies and sleep during the day between rocks, underneath fallen tree trunks or in piles of dead plant material. They make a nest in a bush or in the fork of a branch consisting of a big pile of grass. They are adapted to survive in hot, dry conditions.

Food Omnivorous: feeding on insects, various types of grass and other plant material like protea seeds and herbs.

Breeding 1–7 young are born in the summer.

Mass
±15 g

Length
±26 cm

Age
±2 years

Vocalisation
Squeak

Bushveld gerbil

Tatera leucogaster
(Bosveldse nagmuis)

Mass
±70 g

Length
±28 cm

Age
±5 years

Vocalisation
Long whistles, also low
and high peeps.

Identification The colour of the upperparts varies from reddish-brown to yellowish orange brown. (Animals from the western part of their distribution are paler than those from the east.) The chin, throat and rest of the underparts are white. Behind each eye is a white patch. The hind legs are very long, like those of a kangaroo.
Difference between ♂ and ♀ None.
Habitat Occurs generally on light sandy soils, or sandy alluvium. But sometimes on harder soil in mopaneveld as well, where they do not dig their own burrows, but live in termitaria or in the roots of trees. They live in different habitats, from grassland to woodland.
Habits Nocturnal. The entrance of the burrows, which they dig themselves, is usually under a low bush. At this entrance in the morning is a lot of fresh soil, pushed out during the night. The chambers in these burrows are lined with soft plant material.
Food Green plant material, grass, seeds and insects.
Breeding 1–9 young are born in the nest, any time of the year, but usually in summer.

House rat

Rattus rattus
(Huisrot)

Identification The upperparts of this well-known (introduced) rat varies between shades of grey; the underparts are light grey or white. Its feet are relatively much larger than any of our indigenous rats. The tail is long, about the same length as that of the body.

Difference between ♂ and ♀ None.

Habitat An introduced rat species that occurs widespread in our region, and always close to human activity.

Habits Nocturnal. They sharpen their teeth by gnawing against hard subjects (such as plastic and wood). In this way they create much damage, and become a pest wherever they occur. They make a nest in any suitable shelter and are very fertile.

Food Omnivorous. The white-bellied type is more vegetarian.

Breeding 1–10 young are born anytime of the year. Females produce up to 6 litters a year.

Mass
±98 g

Length
±37 cm

Age
±1 year

Vocalisation
Squeaks

Dung identification

The texture and colour of dung can vary, depending on the food the animal has foraged, and how fresh the droppings are. Dung can also vary according to region. In some regions, antelope even forage on soil as a salt supplement. Predators' dung usually contains more hair – sometimes only hair – and the colour is darker when a lot of blood has been consumed. However, the dung of some predators, such as hyaena, is usually white as a result of its diet.

The texture of dung also varies, especially among smaller predators, but to a lesser extent among antelope. Although the dung of some antelope, such as the waterbuck, usually cakes, this also occurs among other antelope as a variation. During early spring, the dung appears to be softer and caked due to foraging on fresh, green grass and leaf sprouts (see example below).

The photograph below shows the difference between caked and separate droppings of the same animal.

(a) Red duiker (b) Suni (c) Red lechwe (d) Blue wildebeest

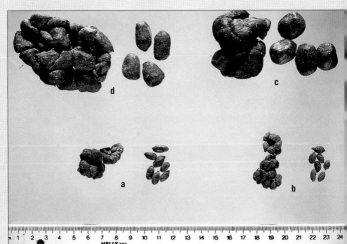

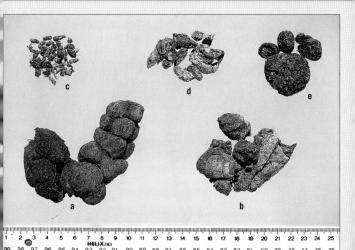

*(a) Chacma baboon (b) Syke's monkey (c) South African galago (d) Greater galago
(e) Vervet monkey*

Chacma baboon Droppings are found in abundance on cliffs and beneath trees in which the baboons sleep.

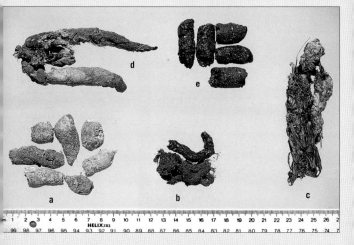

(a) Small spotted cat (b) Polecat (c) Cape fox (d) Small-spotted genet (e) Bat-eared fox

Bat-eared fox Usually defecates close to other dung heaps or sometimes on a common dung heap.

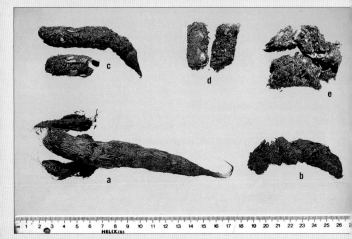

(a) Serval (b) African civet (c) Large-spotted genet (d) Spotted-necked otter
(e) African clawless otter

Serval Defecate without digging or covering dung – only scratches once with hind paws.

African civet Defecate on common dung heaps along their routes.

African clawless otter Dung heaps usually close to the water; contains crab shells.

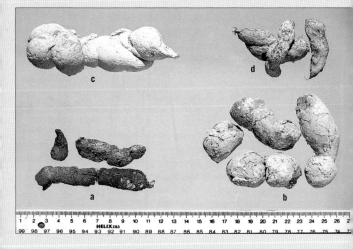

(a) Side-striped jackal (b) Spotted hyaena (c) Brown hyaena (d) Black-backed jackal

Hyaena Droppings of both hyaenas are green when fresh and white when dry. Both make use of common dung heaps, usually close to the boundaries of their territories.

130

(a) African wild cat (b) Aardwolf (c) Honey badger (d) Caracal

African wild cat Digs a small hole and covers the droppings with its front paws.
Aardwolf Defecates on oval dung heaps, first digging a trench and then covering it up.

(a) Leopard (b) Cheetah (c) Lion (d) African wild dog

Leopard Droppings are full of hair and may even contain spines of porcupine.
Cheetah Droppings are usually darker than those of leopard.
Lions Droppings have a distinct scent and are darker in colour – due to the quantity of blood – and may also contain spines of porcupine.

131

(a) Black rhinoceros (b) White rhinoceros (c) Elephant (d) Hippopotamus

Black rhinoceros Usually defecates on a communal dung heap, which it often kicks apart. Dung contains thorns and branches.

White rhinoceros Territorial bulls defecate on dung heaps and often kick them apart. Its dung is dark green when fresh and becomes darker when dry.

Elephant Fresh dung is olive green; turns darker then becomes lighter after 6 hours.

Hippopotamus Usually scatters its dung in or out of the water with a smack of its tail.

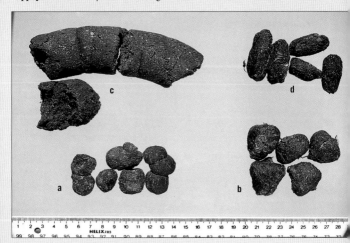

(a) Bushpig (b) Warthog (c) Antbear (d) Porcupine

Antbear Dung contains soil, thus heavy. Digs a shallow hole, defecates and covers up.

(a) Giraffe (b) Buffalo (c) Cape mountain zebra (d) Plains zebra

Giraffe Dung could be confused with that of the kudu, but tends to be more scattered due to the large distance it has to fall.

Buffalo Dung is similar to that of cattle, but is usually darker in colour.

Zebra Dung similar to that of a horse. Mountain zebra droppings larger than plains.

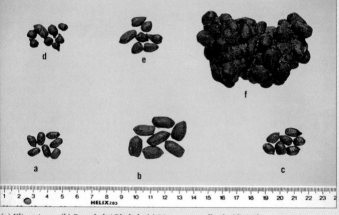

(a) Klipspringer (b) Bontebok / Blesbok (c) Mountain reedbuck (d) Oribi
(e) Grey rhebok (f) Black wildebeest

Klipspringer Defecates on common dung heaps within their territories.

Bontebok / Blesbok Territorial males defecate on dung heaps in their areas.

Black wildebeest (White-tailed gnu) dung is often caked.

133

(a) Greater kudu (b) Nyala (c) Sable antelope (d) Lichtenstein's hartebeest
(e) Roan antelope (f) Tsessebe

(a) Springbok (b) Gemsbok (c) Eland (d) Blue wildebeest
(e) Cape hartebeest (f) Impala

Springbok Territorial males defecate on conspicuous dung heaps in their territory.
Gemsbok Territorial bulls' dung forms small heap because they squat when defecating.
Blue wildebeest Droppings are often caked.
Impala Rams defecate on communal dung heaps (kraals) during the mating season.

(a) Sitatunga (b) Reedbuck (c) Puku (d) Lechwe (e) Waterbuck (f) Bushbuck

Sitatunga Droppings may be caked.

Waterbuck Dung is usually caked.

Bushbuck Dung is often soft and the droppings fall on top of each other.

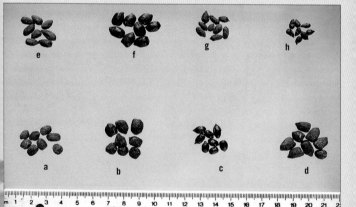

(a) Blue duiker (b) Sharpe's grysbok (c) Steenbok (d) Cape grysbok (e) Red duiker
(f) Common duiker (g) Damara dik-dik

Sharpe's grysbok Likes to defecate on communal dung heaps.

Steenbok Defecates on heaps – mostly on territory border – and usually covers dung.

Damara dik-dik Defecates on communal heaps, usually combined with a form of ritual.

135

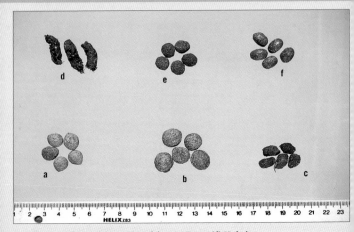

(a) Springhare (b) Scrub hare (c) Rock hyrax / Dassie (d) Hedgehog
(e) Cape hare (f) Greater cane rat

Rock rabbit Droppings are flatter than those of hares and, unlike hares, they usually defecate on common dung heaps some distance from their burrows.

Hyrax/Dassie Usually defecates on common dung heaps, on klipkoppies or in caves.

Greater cane rat Defecates along the paths where it forages.

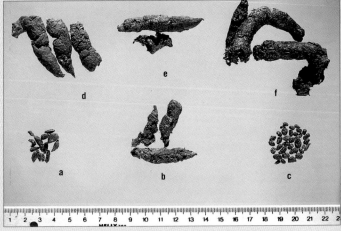

(a) Ground squirrel (b) Yellow mongoose (c) Tree squirrel (d) Banded mongoose
(e) Suricate (meerkat) (f) Marsh mongoose

Mongoose The dung of the different mongooses looks very much alike and it is difficult to distinguish between them.

Spoor identification

Tracking is an art that requires devotion and plenty of practice, and should ideally be learned with the assistance of an expert in the field. This book can therefore only be regarded as an aid. For beginners, however, there are a few hints to bear in mind: the spoor of specific animals may differ in size and shape, depending on the surface on which they have been made. Certain parts of an animal's spoor may be clearly seen in soft or wet soil, but not on hard ground. Hooves, for example, tend to spread wider in wet or muddy soil to ensure better footing.

Identifying spoor using this book

a. Carefully study the spoor charts as well as the area in which the animal can be found.
b. Scan the terrain and compare it to the preferred habitat or the habitat keys.
c. Be on the lookout for other signs close to the animal's spoor (such as droppings, for example) and try to determine on what the animal has foraged. In this way, experts make many interesting observations.

How fresh is the spoor?

a. To determine the freshness of the spoor accurately, keep in mind the weather conditions of the previous few days: was it windless, or was there rain or wind, and if so, exactly when? For example, when tracking a spoor early in the morning, you may remember that the wind blew until about midnight but that the remainder of the night was windless. Then you can determine whether the spoor was made before or after the wind. Use the measurements on the following pages to determine the size of the spoor.
b. Be on the lookout for dung and study it; touch it – if it sticks to your fingers, it is quite fresh, and if it is still warm, it is obviously very fresh. Use the photographs on the previous pages to help identify the dung.

Common mammals

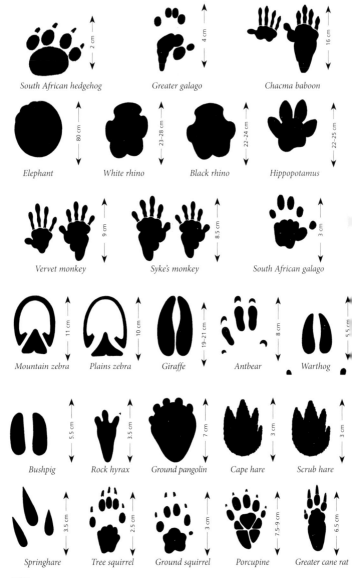

South African hedgehog — 2 cm

Greater galago — 4 cm

Chacma baboon — 16 cm

Elephant — 80 cm

White rhino — 23–28 cm

Black rhino — 22–24 cm

Hippopotamus — 22–25 cm

Vervet monkey — 9 cm

Syke's monkey — 8.5 cm

South African galago — 3 cm

Mountain zebra — 11 cm

Plains zebra — 10 cm

Giraffe — 19–21 cm

Antbear — 8 cm

Warthog — 5.5 cm

Bushpig — 5.5 cm

Rock hyrax — 3.5 cm

Ground pangolin — 7 cm

Cape hare — 3 cm

Scrub hare — 3 cm

Springhare — 3.5 cm

Tree squirrel — 2.5 cm

Ground squirrel — 3 cm

Porcupine — 7.5–9 cm

Greater cane rat — 6.5 cm

Predators

Bat-eared fox — 4 cm

African wild dog — 8.5 cm

Cape fox — 5 cm

Side-striped jackal — 5 cm

Black-backed jackal — 5.5 cm

African clawless otter — 5 cm

Honey badger — 8.5cm

Striped polecat — 2.5 cm

African civet — 5.5 cm

Small-spotted genet — 2.5–3 cm

Large-spotted genet — 2.5–3 cm

Suricate (meerkat) — 3 cm

Yellow mongoose — 2.75 cm

Slender mongoose — 2.5 cm

Cape grey mongoose — 5.5 cm

White-tailed mongoose — 4 cm

Marsh mongoose — 4.5 cm

Banded mongoose

Dwarf mongoose — 5.5 cm

Aardwolf — 5.5 cm

Brown hyaena — 9–10 cm

Spotted hyaena — 9–12 cm

Cheetah — 9–10 cm

Leopard — 7–12 cm

Lion — 13 cm

Caracal — 5 cm

Serval — 4.5 cm

Small spotted cat — 2.5 cm

African wild cat — 4 cm

139

Antelope

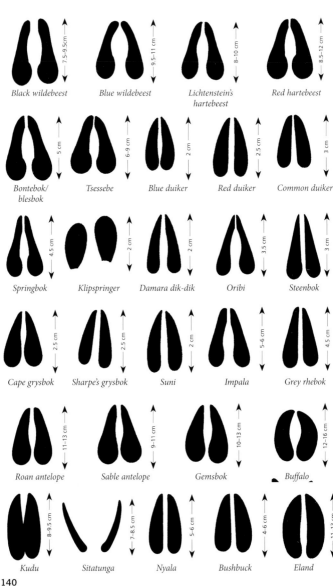

Black wildebeest   7.5–9.5cm

Blue wildebeest   9.5–11 cm

Lichtenstein's hartebeest   8–10 cm

Red hartebeest   8.5–12 cm

Bontebok/ blesbok   5 cm

Tsessebe   6–9 cm

Blue duiker   2 cm

Red duiker   2.5 cm

Common duiker   3 cm

Springbok   4.5 cm

Klipspringer   2 cm

Damara dik-dik   2 cm

Oribi   3.5 cm

Steenbok   3 cm

Cape grysbok   2.5 cm

Sharpe's grysbok   2.5 cm

Suni   2 cm

Impala   5–6 cm

Grey rhebok   4.5 cm

Roan antelope   11–13 cm

Sable antelope   9–11 cm

Gemsbok   10–13 cm

Buffalo   12–16 cm

Kudu   8–9.5 cm

Sitatunga   7–8.5 cm

Nyala   5–6 cm

Bushbuck   4–6 cm

Eland   11–13 cm

Antelope *(continued)*

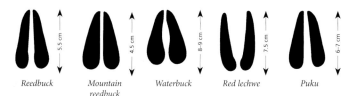

Reedbuck — 5.5 cm

Mountain reedbuck — 4.5 cm

Waterbuck — 8-9 cm

Red lechwe — 7.5 cm

Puku — 6-7 cm

Bibliography

Bronner, G.N., Hoffmann, M., Taylor, P.J., Chimamba, C.T., Best, P.B., Matthee, C.A. & Robinson, T.J. 2003. *A Revised Systematic Checklist of the Extant Mammals of the Southern African Subregion*. Durban: Durban Museum.

Bryant, L. 1989. *Rowland Ward's African Records of Big Game* (xxii edition). San Antonio, Texas: Rowland Ward Publications, a division of Game Conservation International.

Cillié, B. 1997. *The Mammal Guide of Southern Africa*. Pretoria: Briza Publications.

De Graaff, G. 1987. *Diere van die Nasionale Krugerwildtuin*. Cape Town: Struik Publishers.

Dorst, J. & Dandelot, P. 1972. *A Field Guide to the Larger Mammals of Africa*. London: Collins.

Meester, J.A.J. & Setzer, H.W. 1977. *The Mammals of Africa: An Identification Manual*. Washington, D.C.: Smithsonian Institutional Press.

Meester, J.A.J. & Rautenbach, I.L. 1986. *Classification of Southern African Mammals*. Pretoria: Transvaal Museum.

Pienaar, U. de V., Joubert, S.C.J., Hall-Martin, A., De Graaff, G. & Rautenbach, I.L. 1987. *Veldgids tot die Soogdiere van die Nasionale Krugerwildtuin*. Cape Town: Struik Publishers.

Pienaar, U. de V., Rautenbach, I.L. & De Graaff, G. 1980. *The Small Mammals of the Kruger National Park*. Pretoria: National Parks Board of South Africa.

Smithers, R.H.N. 1983. *The Mammals of the Southern African Subregion*. Pretoria: University of Pretoria.

Walker, C. 1988. *Signs of the Wild*. Cape Town: Struik Publishers.

Index

Acknowledgements

I want to express my gratitude to Ceri Prenter and Sunbird Publishers for making this pocket guide such a big success. Also for the confidence displayed in translating it into German.

I extend my thanks to the various wildlife photographers who made their images available for publication.

Many thanks to Kjeld Kruger for making his excellent dung selection available for photographing.

I am also grateful to the Creator of all these beautiful animals, for the privilege to share a small part of his wonderful creation with other people in this way.

Finally – many thanks to my family and friends for their interest and constructive ideas and suggestions.

Burger Cillié

Photo acknowledgements

Jeff Ash: 37; Daryl Balfour: 97 (right); Anthony Bannister/Gallo Images: 39, 42; Ray Barry: 112; Burger Cillié: 28 (right), 30 (right), 31, 32, 33, 34, 36, 38, 45 (right), 49 (left), 51, 56 (left), 60, 63, 69 (both), 71 (right), 73, 74 (left), 75, 77, 78, 80 (both), 82 (both), 83 (right), 84 (both), 86 (both), 89 (both), 90 (both), 92, 95 (both), 99 (left and top), 100 (both), 101 (both), 102 (right), 103 (both), 104 (both), 106, 108, 110, 117, 127; Lizeth Cillié: 26, 35, 41, 53, 55, 64, 85 (right); Niel Cillié: 25, 27, 28 (left), 29 (both), 30 (left), 43, 44, 45 (left), 46, 49 (right), 50, 54, 56 (right), 57, 61, 62, 65, 67, 70, 71 (left), 72, 74 (right), 76, 79, 81 (both), 83 (left), 85 (left), 87 (both), 88 (both), 91, 93, 94 (both), 96 (both), 98 (both), 99 (right), 102 (left), 111, 113, 116, 119, 120, 123; Nigel Dennis: 105; Clem Haagner: 40, 52, 107, 109; Arthur Hall: 115; Martin Harvey/Gallo Images: 58; Lex Hes: 97 (left); Luke Hunter/Gallo Images: 47; Jeanette Matheus: 68; Eric Riesinger: 48; SANParks: 59, 66; Naas Rautenbach: 114, 118, 121, 122, 124, 125, 126